HEMINGWAY

HEMINGWAY

THE
TORONTO YEARS

WILLIAM BURRILL

DOUBLEDAY CANADA LIMITED

Canadian Cataloguing in Publication Data
Hemingway, Ernest, 1899–1961
Hemingway : the Toronto years
Articles written for the Toronto star in the 1920s.
ISBN 0-385-25489-X
I. Burrill, William, 1954–   . II. Title.
PS3515.E37A6 1994 818.5208 C94-931372-6

Cover and text design by Tania Craan
Printed and bound in the USA
Printed on acid-free paper

Published in Canada by
Doubleday Canada Limited
105 Bond Street, Toronto,
Ontario M5B 1Y3

For my father, Scott Burrill, my mother Vivienne
and my wife Heather Moffat
And for William McGeary

CONTENTS

Acknowledgments

HEMINGWAY: THE TORONTO YEARS IS BUILT ON THE HARD work of many Hemingway scholars. Previous books focusing on Hemingway and Toronto are acknowledged in my introduction. But in addition to these, my sources include the works that cover Hemingway's entire life, especially Carlos Baker's *Ernest Hemingway: Selected Letters* (New York: Charles Scribner's Sons, 1981); Jeffrey Meyers, *Hemingway: A Biography* (New York: Harper & Row, 1985); Kenneth S. Lynn, *Hemingway* (New York: Simon & Schuster, 1987); James R. Mellow, *Hemingway: A Life without Consequences* (New York: Houghton Mifflin Company, 1992); and Denis Brian, *The True Gen* (New York: Grove Press, 1988). I am particularly indebted to the writers who specialized in Hemingway's younger years, especially Morley Callaghan, *That Summer in Paris* (New York: Penguin Books, 1963); Michael S. Reynolds, *The Young Hemingway* (New York: Basil Blackwell, 1986) and *Hemingway: The Paris Years* (Cambridge, Mass.: Basil Blackwell, 1989); Giola Diliberto, *Hadley* (New York: Ticknor & Fields, 1992); Peter Griffin, *Along with Youth* (New York: Oxford University Press, 1985); Leicester Hemingway, *My Brother, Ernest Hemingway* (Cleveland: World, 1962); Scott Donaldson, *By Force of Will: The Life and Art of Ernest Hemingway* (New York: Viking, 1977) and also Donaldson's article, "Hemingway of the Star" from *Ernest Hemingway: The Papers of a Writer*, ed. Bernard Oldsey (New York: Garland, 1981).

Other sources include memoirs and histories of the *Toronto Star*, most notably Ross Harkness, *J.E. Atkinson of The Star* (Toronto: University of Toronto Press, 1963); Jock Carroll, *The Life and Times of Greg Clark* (Toronto: Doubleday Canada, 1981); J.H. Cranston, *Ink on My Fingers* (Toronto: The Ryerson Press, 1953) and Roy Greenaway, *The News Game* (Toronto: Clarke, Irwin, 1966).

Most importantly, I am indebted to the John F. Kennedy Library in Boston for the generous use of their Hemingway files, materials and photographs, Princeton University Library for access to their Carlos Baker Collection, the City of Toronto Archives for the use of photographs and the *Toronto*

Star for permission to use their archives, library, photographs and the right to reprint the Hemingway *Toronto Star* articles.

I would like to extend special thanks to my agent Beverley Slopen for her belief in this book; to publisher John Honderich and assistant managing editor Michael Peiri of the *Toronto Star* for allowing me the freedom to pursue this project while I was a *Star* editor; to Andrew Go, Steve Jarrett and Bill Reynolds of *eye Weekly* for bearing with me; to John Pearce, Maggie Reeves and Susan Folkins of Doubleday Canada for their support, patience and invaluable advice; and to Lang and Norma Moffat for the use of the cabin in which most of this book was written (I'll clean it up later — I promise).

Introduction

THE BIOGRAPHICAL DETAILS OF HEMINGWAY'S TORONTO years have all the ingredients of a novel — a young hero, colorful adventures, a meteoric rise, intrigue and double-dealing and a final fall at the hands of an adversary bent on cutting a "prima donna" down to size. My goal in writing this book is not only to produce the first critical biography to focus on Ernest Hemingway's four-year association with the city of Toronto and the *Toronto Star* newspaper but also to present a collection of "lost" stories written by Hemingway for the *Toronto Star*, and reveal for the first time that, while in Toronto, Hemingway secretly wrote for two of the *Star*'s rivals, the *Globe* and the *Mail and Empire*. It is also my purpose to examine how Hemingway's Toronto affiliation contributed to his development into one of the most famous American writers of the twentieth century.

Although Hemingway had brief experience as a cub reporter for the *Kansas City Star* in 1917, the work he produced there consisted of short spot news reports that were mostly telephoned to a rewrite desk. Hemingway never received a byline during his eight months on the *Kansas City Star*, and while he no doubt learned something from the discipline of churning out routine "5-W" formula news reports, the Kansas City stories that have been identified as Hemingway's show no signs of his later distinctive style. It was not until he began working for the *Toronto Star* in 1920 that Hemingway was awarded his first bylines and allowed to write the kind of feature material that was closer to fiction than to hard news. Although Hemingway would later dismiss his journalism as unimportant, he was proud enough of his *Star* work at the time to mail it to family and friends, carry sample clippings in his wallet and carefully preserve each story in scrapbooks, which he saved until the end of his life. And although Hemingway's parents tried to push him into college, he told his friends that the way to become a fiction writer was not through school but through newspaper work. Indeed, most of his literary heroes of the period, including Stephen Crane, Ring Lardner,

Mark Twain, George Ade and Jack London, had started out as newspaper reporters.

Hemingway's Toronto journalism is obviously not of the same caliber as his meticulously crafted works of fiction, but much of it is distinctive in its own right. As his *Toronto Star* career progresses from 1920 to 1924, one can see the development of his literary style. The *Star* gave Hemingway the chance not only to write whatever he wanted but also to roam Europe as a foreign correspondent. It was for the *Star* that Hemingway first wrote about bullfights, bohemians, battles, booze, bass and many of the other topics that would later appear in his fiction. By the time Hemingway had left Toronto and the *Star*, he had published his first two volumes of fiction — *Three Stories & Ten Poems* and *in our time*.

For the purpose of this book, I have defined Hemingway's "Toronto years" as beginning on January 8, 1920, when he arrived to live in Toronto for the first time, and ending on January 19, 1924, the day his last *Star* article appeared and also the day Hemingway and his wife, Hadley, sailed for Paris. Hemingway lived in Toronto only for four months at the beginning of this period and another four months at the end, but he had a connection to the city during the middle period through his almost continual work for the *Toronto Star* as a

freelance writer, then a European correspondent
and finally a staff reporter. This book concentrates
most heavily on the early 1920 period and the late
1923 period when Hemingway was a Toronto resident, because no other biography has done so.
I have condensed the middle period, when Hemingway returned to Chicago and later moved to
Paris as a *Star* correspondent; other books have
covered this period so thoroughly that there is little
left to add. I have uncovered, however, additional
stories and other material from this middle period
as well as from the early and late periods.

A number of Hemingway's *Star* articles were
published in *By-line: Ernest Hemingway* (New York:
Charles Scribner's Sons, 1967), edited by William
White. Later, White gathered and published all the
known *Toronto Star* material, whether bylined, unsigned or written under pen names, in the collection *Dateline, Toronto: The Complete Toronto
Star Dispatches, 1920–1924*, also published by
Scribner's in 1985. This book is an invaluable collection of 172 *Star* pieces attributed to Hemingway.
It includes everything from long essays to short,
unsigned, one-paragraph cables.

During my research, I found thirty additional
Hemingway *Toronto Star* stories that are not included in the so-called complete *Dateline, Toronto*
collection as well as one unknown story from the

Globe and two from the *Mail and Empire.* These discoveries had their beginning when I read the files of the late *Star* librarian William McGeary, who had identified 158 of the 172 stories that appear in *Dateline, Toronto.* McGeary made a life work of Hemingway scholarship and was the main source of *Toronto Star* information for the most famous of all Hemingway biographies, Carlos Baker's *Ernest Hemingway: A Life Story* (New York: Charles Scribner's Sons, 1969). McGeary's files in the *Toronto Star* library included not only invaluable source material but also five more stories that McGeary had identified as the work of Hemingway but that are not included in *Dateline, Toronto.* McGeary's five "lost" stories got me started, and by the time I had finished poring over microfiche in the *Star* library and searching through Hemingway's papers at John F. Kennedy Library in Boston, I had found twenty-five more stories that are missing from the "complete" collection. No doubt other researchers knew of the existence of some of these stories. Yet all are missing from the official record of Hemingway's Toronto output and none has been published in book form until now.

Many books have been written about Ernest Hemingway, but no other critical biography has focused exclusively on his Toronto connection. Although not exclusively about Hemingway in Toronto Charles Fenton's *The Apprenticeship of Ernest Hemingway: The Early Years* (New York: Viking Press, 1954), included an excellent analysis of Hemingway's early work for the *Kansas City Star* and the *Toronto Star*. I found this book extremely useful in my research. Indeed, Fenton did such a good job analyzing Hemingway's Toronto works that many other scholars have pointedly skimmed over the period, feeling that it was covered. But Fenton's book was written forty years ago and is unfortunately now long out of print. Furthermore, there is now much material that Fenton did not know about when he wrote his book. So a new look at the Toronto period is in order. Two works by David Donnell, *Hemingway in Toronto* (Toronto: Black Moss, 1982) and *The Blue Ontario Hemingway Boat Race* (Toronto: Coach House, 1985) are fictional tributes to Hemingway but neither is a critical biography.

Interest in Hemingway remains high. The Encyclopedia Britannica's Instant Research Center in Chicago fields more than 170,000 questions from the public each year. On their "Most Asked About List," Hemingway ranks fourth, behind John F. Kennedy, William Shakespeare and Sigmund Freud. The most frequently asked question about Hemingway is how he came to develop his prose style.

With *Hemingway: The Toronto Years*, I aim to present new research and new stories that will answer many of those who, where, what and when questions.

And, most important, why.

Ticket to Toronto, 1919

BY THE SUMMER OF 1919 THE GREAT WAR IN EUROPE WAS over. Ernest Hemingway had been badly wounded while serving as a Red Cross ambulance driver in Italy a year before. Now that he was home he spent his days upstairs in his room, working on his fiction writing, drinking from the bottles he kept hidden behind his books. "I go over to the camouflaged book case in my room," he wrote to James Gamble, a friend he met in Italy, "and pour out a very stiff tall one and add the conventional amount of aqua and set it by my typewriter."[1] After his first taste of Europe, Hemingway hated the stifling temperance of suburban Oak Park, Illinois, where lawns were wide and minds were narrow. His father, Dr. Clarence Hemingway, had begun suggesting that it was time Ernest went to school

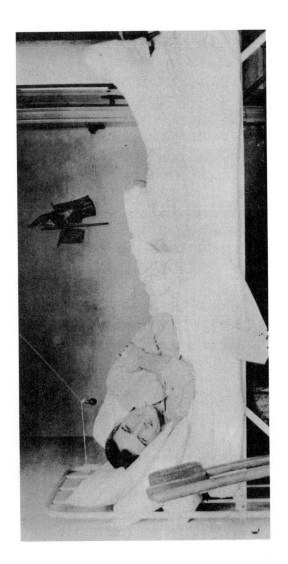

Recuperating from his war wounds at the Red Cross Hospital in Milan, Italy, in July 1918, Hemingway put on a brave face for the camera. But he would soon be wounded again, this time by a rejection from Red Cross nurse Agnes Von Kurowsky, whom he had hoped to marry.

(Henry Villard collection)

or found a real job, but lately, Clarence's increasing depressions had left him incapable of asserting himself about much of anything. It was Ernest's mother, Grace, who had become the dominant member of the household. At first she had doted over her injured son, but by now he'd had a year to recover and he could not use his wounds as an excuse forever. He would be twenty years old in July, and although he had worked hard at his writing for a year, he had not sold a single story. Grace insisted it was time that Ernest stopped his moping and got an education. "My family, God bless them as always, are wolfing at me to go to college," Ernest wrote to his friend Lawrence T. Barnett that spring. "They want me to settle down for a while and the place that they are pulling for very strong is Wisconsin [University]. I don't know anything about it except that there is nobody of the male sex worth a damn that goes there. . . . However I know there are some very priceless femmes go there. . . . Frankly I don't know where the hell to go."[2]

Hemingway had four sisters and a young brother. His sisters, Marcelline, Ursula and Sunny (Madelaine), would bring him food as he lay in his room, working on his stories. "One of the Kid sisters just brought up a plate of lobster salad sandwiches," he wrote to Gamble, "the inference being

Hemingway returned from World War I in a dress uniform he had had specially tailored in Italy in 1918, complete with military insignia he was not entitled to wear — having never been an official combatant in the war — and without any trace of Red Cross insignia. (John F. Kennedy Library)

that fish is brain food I guess. But they need Beer." In return for the room service, Hemingway would offer his sisters nips from his hidden bottles and puffs from his cigars. "Smoke that, Kid," he told fourteen-year-old Sunny, "and we'll be friends again." He taught his sisters all the Italian swear words and dirty songs he had learned.[3]

After a morning of writing, he would put on his Italian uniform and wander around Oak Park. He gave speeches about his war experiences at local clubs and invited his ambulance service friends to drinking parties. He was welcomed home as a hero, but privately, he knew his war stories were becoming more and more exaggerated. "They tried to make a hero out of me," he told Gamble. "But you know and I know that all the real heroes are dead. If I had been a really game guy, I would have gotten myself killed off."

His favorite sister, Ursula, seventeen, would wait up for him when he came home from a drinking session and help him to his room. He would sleep with the light on, as he often did since the war injury, and sometimes Ursula would sleep with him, as he said, "so I would not be lonely at night." He worked on his stories and wrote letters to friends, bragging of his drinking prowess. "Your old pal Hem established the club record, 18 martinis, 3 champagne highballs and I don't know how much champagne, then I passed out," he told his ambulance service friend Howell Jenkins that June, describing a party at the Toledo Club. "It was a wonderful occasion. The night Toledo went dry."[4]

When the family left Oak Park in July for their annual two-month vacation at their Walloon Lake cottage near Petoskey, Michigan, Hemingway carried with him a suitcase full of short stories and sketches that, so far, not even a luggage thief would take. The rejections from the magazines piled up on top of the rejection letter he'd received from Agnes Von Kurowsky, an American nurse, eight years older than Ernest, whom Hemingway had fallen in love with while in hospital in Milan the summer before. From Milan, Ernest had written his best friend, Bill Smith, telling him of his new fiancée, and asking Smith to be the best man at the wedding. "Why man I've only got about 50 more years to live and I don't want to waste any of them, and every minute that I'm away from that Kid is wasted," Ernest wrote. "Now try to keep your finger off the trigger cause you may be in the same fix yourself some day."[5] But in March of 1919, after Hemingway had returned home, Agnes wrote to break the news that she was in love with an Italian officer closer to her own age, and expected to marry him soon. She took all the blame, adding,

"But I am now and always will be too old and that's the truth and I can't get away from the fact that you are just a boy — a kid."[6] Hemingway would never forget Agnes. (She bears a striking resemblance to the character of the nurse Catherine Barkley in *A Farewell to Arms*.) But over the summer of 1919, he tried to erase her from memory by pursuing Bill Smith's sister Katy, who was exactly eight years his senior. Katy Smith would not be the last "older woman" to catch Ernest's eye.

That summer Grace Hemingway opened her own private cottage that she had had built despite the objections of her husband. Grace Cottage, as she named it, was a mile across the lake from the family cottage, Windemere. There Grace stayed with her two youngest children, Carol, eight, and Leicester, four, and her companion, Ruth Arnold. Hemingway had taken his father's side in the argument over the cottage, saying his mother's vain extravagance had used up the money that was to send him to college. This was untrue. Grace Hemingway built the cottage with her own money from an inheritance, and Ernest clearly had no intention of going to college. But like any story of Hemingway's, he stuck to it.

At the cottage, the friction between mother and son increased because, for the first time since

*Ernest, twenty years old, spent the uneasy summer of
1919 at the Hemingway cottage at Walloon Lake,
Michigan. While he struggled to write fiction, his
parents felt it was time he either went to college or
found a real job.* (John F. Kennedy Library)

Ernest was an infant, Dr. Hemingway had chosen to stay in Oak Park for the summer. Ernest blamed his mother for his father's depressions and withdrawal from family life. He decided that if his father would no longer stand up to Grace, then he would do the job himself. Although Grace expected him to help with daily domestic chores, Ernest kept far away from Grace Cottage, staying at Horton Bay with Bill and Katy Smith, fishing, swimming and drinking with his summer friends. When he did show up at the cottage, it was often with a group who would stay for dinner. Grace complained in a letter to her husband that although the extra work had caused her arthritis to flare up, Ernest did not seem sympathetic. His sister Marcelline, a year older, began taking her mother's side in the arguments, which sparked a whole new round of battles.

By the end of the summer, it was clear from Dr. Hemingway's obsessive daily letters that, despite the time alone in Oak Park, his depressions and mood swings were worse than ever. Family tension increased when Dr. Hemingway suddenly wrote to ban Grace's companion, Ruth, from the Hemingway home, even though Ruth had lived with the family for more than a decade. It was clear that Dr. Hemingway now regarded Ruth as not a mere companion to his wife, but a rival. While Marcelline said her father was "insane on the subject" of Ruth,[7] Ernest backed his father. If Dr. Hemingway had become unbalanced, it was Grace's fault, he decided. And he too suspected the nature of Grace's relationship with Ruth; many years later he would ban his own son from visiting Grace because she was "androgynous." Biographers continue to debate the real story behind these family feuds, but it is clear that, for Ernest Hemingway, home was not a pleasant place in 1919.

Faced with the prospect of a return to such a family atmosphere in Oak Park, Ernest decided to stay up in Michigan when the family cottage was closed for the winter. He took a cheap rooming house in nearby Petoskey. He wrote every day, bombarding the top-priced *Saturday Evening Post* with clumsy attempts at the kind of slick magazine fiction that was paying hot young writers like F. Scott Fitzgerald as much as $500 a short story. He tried to write about the underbelly of gangland Chicago, but he had no experience in the subject. His stories did not ring true, the style was awkward, the prose purple and the dialogue contrived. In one of those stories, a hard-boiled Chicago gangster is sent to kill a rival gang member named Pinky Miller. The thug finds Pinky in his favorite bar, pulls a gun and says, "Somebody's due for a one-way trip to that land out of which's bourn no travelers return. You ain't afraid to die, are you, Pinky?" As biographer Michael Reynolds aptly notes, "The young Hemingway could not resist mixing Ring Lardner in with his Kipling and Shakespeare."[8]

Not surprisingly, his numerous submissions to the *Saturday Evening Post* bounced back with alarming speed and without comment. Hemingway tried lowering his sights and his expectations, but not even *Redbook* or *Popular Magazine* would give him a chance. With no other source of income, he lived off an insurance payment he had received after his war wounding. But as winter approached, the insurance money was nearly all gone. Ernest tried to say afloat by working part time, shoveling gravel for the county — not easy work for a man whose right leg still stiffened and ached with exercise.

As the new year and the new decade approached, Hemingway had two options: return home to Oak Park and admit defeat, or find a job that would allow him the time and money to continue with his dream of becoming a writer. But where? Doing what? Good jobs were hard to find with two million veterans out of work in the stale postwar economy, and he had no college education. Yet Hemingway, as he would throughout his life, always had a knack for being in the right place at the right time. Just when things looked their bleakest, along came a highly unlikely job offer.

It came out of a chance meeting with Harriet Gridley Connable of Toronto, who owned a cottage near the Hemingway place. In the fall of 1919, Mrs. Connable had happened to attend a meeting of the Petoskey Ladies Auxiliary Club, at which a young veteran named Ernest Hemingway was a guest speaker. Hemingway, handsome in his Italian military cloak and high boots, thrilled his audience with a detailed, gory and highly exaggerated account of his war wounding in Italy.

The facts of Hemingway's war wounding are somewhat inglorious: Ernest was a Red Cross volunteer, taking chocolate bars to the Italian soldiers stationed at the front in the Piave district. He was not an official combatant in this war (nor would he ever be in any other war). As he was distributing the chocolate and cigarettes to troops in an observation post beyond the front lines, the Austrian enemy troops lobbed over an antipersonnel trench mortar — a gallon drum filled with explosives, slugs and scrap metal. The shell scored a direct hit, exploding in the trench and blowing the legs off the soldier next to Hemingway. Although the soldier died instantly and absorbed most of the blast, hundreds of shards of shrapnel ripped into Ernest's right leg. Stretcher bearers carried him back to the trenches. He woke up in a Milan army hospital not knowing if his leg would be saved. After weeks of recovery, and after falling in love with the nurse Agnes Von Kurowsky, Hemingway was awarded two medals of valor by the Italians, who were eager to create an American hero to bolster U.S. support for their war. He was shipped home to a hero's welcome. He had been brave enough: he had gone to the front knowing the danger, and he had almost died. There was nothing wrong with the story. It was simply that — then as later in his life — Ernest Hemingway could not help improving a story. Especially one in which he was cast as the hero. He immediately began fertilizing tales of his war experiences, first in letters home, then in statements to reporters and finally in the speech that brought him to the Petoskey women's group. By this point he had promoted himself from Red Cross volunteer to an officer in the Arditi shock troops, an Italian infantry unit made up of murderers and arsonists who had been granted release on the condition that they fight for their country. The Arditi forces were essentially cannon fodder, carrying revolvers, grenades and short swords as they rushed headlong to almost certain death against impossible odds.

*Long after he returned from the Great War,
Hemingway continued to wear his Italian military
cap, cape and officer's boots. It was in this uniform
that he gave a speech to a Petoskey, Michigan,
women's club meeting attended by Harriet Connable
of Toronto. She was so impressed that she hired him
on the spot to baby-sit her semi-invalid son, Ralph
Jr. (John F. Kennedy Library)*

It is not hard to see why young Hemingway would find it more romantic to be associated with these desperate, fearless and oddly honorable soldiers than to admit that he had suffered his near-mortal wounds as a Red Cross volunteer handing out candy to the real soldiers.

By the time Mrs. Connable heard Hemingway's war tale, he had completely reinvented himself. He gave his speech dressed in infantry boots, cloak and hat featuring insignia he was not entitled to wear. He brandished "captured" weapons and even his blood-soaked and shrapnel-riddled pants.

> When [the mortar shell] exploded, it seemed as if I was moving somewhere in a sort of red din. I said to myself, "Gee! Stein, you're dead!" and then I began to feel myself pulling back to earth. Then I woke up. The sand bags had caved in on my legs and at first I felt disappointed that I had not been wounded. The other soldiers had retreated leaving me and several others for dead. One of the soldiers who was left started crying. So I knew he was alive and told him to shut up. The Austrians seemed determined to wipe out this one outpost. They had star shells out and their trench searchlights were trying to locate us. I picked up the

wounded man and started back toward the trenches. As I got up to walk my kneecap felt warm and sticky, so I knew I'd been touched. Just before we reached the trench their search-light spotted us and they turned a machine-gun on us. One got me in the thigh. It felt like a snowball, so hard and coming with such force that it knocked me down. We started on, but just as we reached the trench and were about to jump in, another bullet hit me, this time in the foot. It tumbled me and my wounded man all in a heap in the trench and when I came to again I was in a dugout. Two soldiers had come to the conclusion that I was to "pass out shortly" [die]. By some arguing, I was able to convince them that they were wrong.[9]

Connable was so impressed with Hemingway's speech that she approached him afterwards. She explained that he was just the sort of young man she and her husband, Ralph Connable Sr., were looking for. Would he like to come to work for them in Toronto over the coming winter?

Many would try to buy Hemingway's friendship over the coming decades of mythic fame. And many would later pay for having been his friend. But when Hemingway decided to come to Toronto in January of 1920, it would be the only time his companionship was purchased with cost and conditions spelled out clearly in advance. His function, if he accepted the Toronto assignment, would be to serve as a glorified baby-sitter — as paid companion for nineteen-year-old Ralph Connable Jr., a partially crippled and apathetic son of wealthy department store mogul Ralph Senior, who planned to take the rest of his family south to Florida for the winter. The Connables felt that the robust and athletic Ernest would be the perfect role model for the sickly Ralph.

As Ralph Senior wrote in the letter outlining Hemingway's job description:

> You [are] to make your home at our house, devote your time to your literary studies and work undisturbed. The work you would do for me would be by your talks and association, to give Ralph the right slant on life, especially as to his sports and pleasures . . . I wanted to be sure that he had the right companionship in the evenings, and my plan was to supply you with the necessary funds to pay for such entertainments and sports as you felt would lead him along the right channel. The fact that he has never taken much interest in athletics is due to an injury he sustained at birth, and

his right hand and limb are not fully developed — they are in length but not in strength,
and I was very anxious to get someone to interest him in athletics so he would overcome
this handicap.[10]

Baby-sitting was hardly Hemingway's idea of
suitable job, but he had his own reasons for looking at the Toronto job as a perfect opportunity,
as a needed escape. The Connables promised him
the free run of an impressive mansion for the winter and encouraged the young man to use the freedom to pursue his career as a writer. After learning
that Hemingway had worked for eight months as
a cub reporter for the *Kansas City Star* before going
to war, Mr. Connable — who had clout as a major
newspaper advertiser — also promised to try to
get Hemingway a job on the *Toronto Star*, which
was emerging as Ontario's biggest and most ag-
gressive newspaper.

Just before the Christmas of 1919, Hemingway
wrote to his friend Howell Jenkins, "This Toronto
thing looks like the original Peruvian Doughnuts."[11] He was referring to a bit of slang from
one of his early short stories. There is no direct
translation, but the meaning is clear. "This Toronto
thing" was no mere job offer. It was like the last
lifeboat off the *Titanic*.

CHAPTER 1

Hemingway the Baby-sitter, 1920

ERNEST HEMINGWAY'S FIRST GLIMPSE OF TORONTO WAS FROM the west as the train followed along the frozen north shore of Lake Ontario. In the year 1920 the flat, widespread city was spiked with countless Gothic spires, which gave it its two nicknames, the City of Churches and, by extension, Toronto the Good. It was the coldest January in decades and the snow almost reached the power wires that hung in webs over the frozen streets. The old Toronto train station was drafty, cold and obsolete. Although the grand Union Station stood newly completed across the street, its opening had been delayed by one important fact — there were no train tracks. (The exact placement of the tracks would keep Toronto politicians squabbling and delay the opening of the station for seven more years.)

Toronto was a flat, sprawling city spiked with church spires when Hemingway arrived in January 1920. The Connable mansion that would be Hemingway's home was located on the hill in the background, on what were then the city limits. (City of Toronto Archives)

As he climbed down onto the station platform, Hemingway was careful to disguise his limp. It had been only a few months earlier that, while climbing down from another train, he had been shocked to hear a railway worker call out, "Hold her up. There's a cripple and he needs time to get his stuff down."[1] He wrapped himself against the cold in his heavy Italian military cloak and, supporting himself with a walking stick, set off to meet the chauffeur and car sent by his new employers. The Connable car pulled away from the station into streets clogged with horse-drawn wagons and streetcars. After passing the squalor of Toronto's waterfront, the car turned north, following Bathurst Street up the hill that Toronto's wealthiest families had staked out as a good spot from which to look down upon a city shaken by postwar poverty and unemployment. Near St. Clair Avenue West, at the city limits, the car turned onto an icy, rutted road, pulling at last into the wide circular driveway of 153 Lyndhurst Avenue. The Connable home was no castle, but it was still one of the most palatial residences in the city, and certainly the biggest house Hemingway had ever been inside. It stood at the top of a hill, overlooking a ravine and the farmland that stretched to the northeast.

Despite the bitter cold outside, the welcome inside was warm as Harriet and Ralph Connable Sr.

greeted Hemingway and took him on a tour. The house had everything — an exercise room with weights, rowing machine and boxing gloves, a music room complete with a huge pipe organ and instruments of every shape and size, a billiards room with low-slung lights, a massive library and an outdoor skating rink, stables and horses. There was also — to Ernest's delight after coming from Prohibition-dry Chicago — a well-stocked collection of liquor in a downstairs vault.

Ralph Junior was presented to Hemingway scrubbed, combed and dressed in his best outfit for the occasion. Even though Ralph was only a couple of months younger than Hemingway's twenty years, the two had little in common. Ernest, dark, handsome, strong, enthusiastic, was everything the lame, introverted youth was not. This, of course, was the very reason that Hemingway had been chosen for the job. The Connables hoped that Ralph would take courage from the fact that Hemingway also suffered from a damaged leg but managed to overcome his disability with good grace and cheer. They hoped some of the Hemingway magic would rub off on their son. Ernest was expected to spend not only his days with young Ralph but also his nights. Although the spacious house had many vacant guest bedrooms, Hemingway was asked to sleep in the same room as Ralph Junior. Ernest was not keen on the idea, but agreed for Mrs. Connable's sake. "I did this for her because I was truly fond of her," he said later.[2]

Soon after Ernest took up his new duties, he received a letter from his father Clarence, who mistakenly assumed that "young Ralph" was just a child. "Write to me often dear boy," Clarence wrote, "and if Ralph needs a walloping, now is the time while his folks are away to pound respect into him."[3] Although Hemingway never did this, it is likely that the thought crossed his mind. He found his reluctant ward to be sickly and apathetic — two traits that Hemingway could not abide. Worse, Ernest soon began thinking of Ralph as a sexually "twisted" kid who preferred burlesque shows at Loews Theatre to outdoor sports and boxing matches. Despite their enforced togetherness, Ernest quickly realized the hopelessness of his task, dismally concluding that "Ralph was no fun."[4]

Although Hemingway had little in common with Ralph, he took an instant liking to the boy's older sister, Dorothy, a short, attractive, dark-eyed brunette who, at twenty-six, had that special allure of being an older woman. Dorothy Connable had also gone overseas in 1918, working for the Red Cross in France, where she established a YMCA for the Sixth Division. After the war, Dorothy spent time in Germany, offering aid to the army of occupation. She and Hemingway hit it off instantly.

"When we met for the first time it was on a stairway landing, where we talked for an hour before realizing he was going somewhere up and I down," Dorothy later recalled. "When together we talked, the topics were endless. His experiences in Italy and mine in France, politics, plays, his newspaper assignments, cartoons, books and everything else." The talk of books especially excited Hemingway. He would rush out and buy her copies of the books he loved. He gave her O. Henry's *Cabbages and Kings*, signing it "To the Negative from the Affirmative." He gave her a copy of Gabriele D'Annunzio's *The Flame*, complete with an inscription that absolved her from blame for owning it and putting the responsibility on himself.[5]

During one of their long chats up in her room, Hemingway told Dorothy that they were both "very young old soldiers." Despite his wounds, Hemingway was still enthusiastic about his wartime experiences, and the war-glorifying Italian novelist D'Annunzio was the postwar writer he most admired. Only a year later, as he turned bitter about the "glory" of war, he would savage this same author in a short poem:

The Connable mansion at 153 Lyndhurst Avenue had a music room, a skating rink, stables and even a large, well-stocked liquor vault in the cellar. It was the home of Ralph Connable Sr., the head of the Canadian chain of Woolworths department stores. Although there were many bedrooms, Ernest shared a room with nineteen-year-old Ralph Jr., whom he had been paid to mind during the winter of 1920.
(*Toronto Star* photo)

D'ANNUNZIO

Half a million dead wops

And he got a kick out of it

The son of a bitch.[6]

The Connable home was on what was at that time the northern boundary of the city, with plenty of wide-open spaces for sports. Hemingway joined Dorothy and her friends in tobogganing, skiing and snow-shoeing in the ravine. When they stopped to rest, Hemingway impressed his new Canadian friends with his outdoor skills, even brushing away the snow and making a fire, and bringing out bread and cheese for all. "He could always heighten a good moment," Dorothy recalled.[7]

Hemingway's future wife would later label Dorothy Connable a dangerous rival. But Hemingway showed particular interest in an attractive friend of Dorothy's named Bonnie Bonnell, a six-foot-tall brunette who often joined him in outdoor adventures. Bonnell was not only beautiful but a relative of the famous and wealthy Masseys, who spawned the Hollywood actor Raymond Massey and endowed the Massey Hall concert facility. Together Bonnie and Ernest formed their own private club, the Bathurst Street Hunt Club, with a membership of two. Ernest would take her horseback riding up unpaved Bathurst Street and out through the open country north and west of the city limits, and what they were hunting for was their secret. Unable to bend his injured knee to fit his feet into the stirrups of the English saddle, Hemingway rode awkwardly, with both legs dangling straight out.

His job had its good points. It gave Hemingway plenty of time to write, since Ralph had morning classes and worked at one of his father's department stores during the afternoons. And when Hemingway got lonely for a familiar face, he could call on his Petoskey pal Dutch Pailthrop, who was also in Toronto for the winter, working in one of the Connables' five-and-dime stores. And although Ralph Junior had proved to be no fun, his father was just the opposite. Hemingway took an instant liking to the senior Connable. He may have lived in opulence in his mansion on the hill, but he was no snob. Connable came from a poor family that had lived beside the stockyards of Chicago, and he had created his own wealth and social status by moving to Toronto in 1915 to expand the Canadian Woolworths department-store chain from ten to one hundred stores. Now, even though he moved in the richest and most powerful circles of Toronto society, he remained, as his more discreet friends would put it, an eccentric.

The elder Connable's pranks soon became the talk of the town. Once, while entertaining the Eaton family, owners of Toronto's biggest department store, Connable excused himself and secretly returned among the servants, dressed as a butler in a long black beard. With the next course, he returned wearing an even longer blue beard. The Eatons said nothing. By the third course, the mysterious servant was now wearing flaming red whiskers that hung all the way to the floor, a beard so bushy that the doddering butler could barely see where he was walking. The guests were fast becoming uncomfortable until Lady Eaton recognized her host and burst into laughter. Connable liked to answer the door wearing huge false buck teeth. He was also known to dress as a woman and prance into the men's locker room at the exclusive Lambton Golf Club. As the men shouted and fumbled to cover their private parts, Connable would grab one and urgently whisper, "I'm looking for my gentleman friend."[8]

Hemingway admired both Mr. Connable's warped sense of humor and his straight shooting with a pool cue. In the early part of his stay, Hemingway regularly lost close but decisive snooker games — and wagers that left him complaining that his new boss was winning back all the money he was to pay Hemingway for minding Ralph Junior.

Although Ralph Connable Sr. found Hemingway to be "modest, sensitive and wonderfully considerate guest,"[9] Ernest was not above a few eccentric schemes of his own. One day he found some strange numbers etched on a post along Lyndhurst Avenue, close to the Connable house. Farther along he found more strange numbers, which he decoded to mean that a plot was afoot to blow up the Connable mansion. He charged back and urged the Connables to procure four machine-guns and mount them at every corner of the house to give a taste of hot lead to the conspirators. Mrs. Connable somehow managed to talk him out of the battle plan and sent him back to his typewriter for the even bigger fight ahead: getting published.

Ernest soon reminded the elder Connable of his promise to try to get him some newspaper work on the *Toronto Star*. Connable asked a friend, Arthur Donaldson, the *Star*'s display advertising manager, to take Ernest around to meet the appropriate editors and see if Hemingway and the *Star* had any future together.

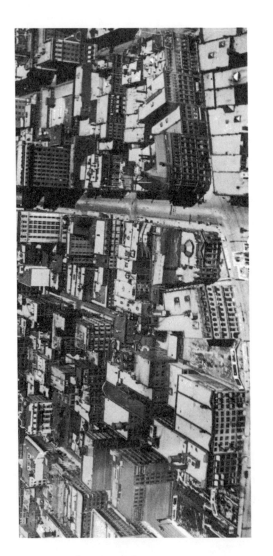

Downtown Toronto was dominated in 1920 by the 19- and 20-story bank buildings at "Skyscraper Corner," at King and Yonge Streets (middle of photo), only steps from the Toronto Star office. Star editorials from the period fretted that such unnaturally high buildings would cause strong wind currents that would carry pedestrians away.

(City of Toronto Archives)

CHAPTER 2

Just Another Hanger-on

THE *TORONTO STAR* OF 1920 WAS ALREADY EMERGING AS NOT just the biggest paper in a five-newspaper city but also one of the scrappiest (and some suggested dropping the *S*) sheets to be found anywhere in North America. The dingy four-story *Star* building at 18–20 King Street West wasn't much to look at but it was just a few doors away from the architectural marvels of "Skyscraper Corner" at the intersection of King and Yonge Streets. Here two bank buildings towered over Toronto, including one that soared a full twenty stories. The *Star* was proud of these symbols of Toronto's emerging cosmopolitanism, and was quick to point out in its pages that visitors to this corner were standing before the "tallest buildings in all of Canada, all of the British empire." One *Star* story, headlined

In 1920 the Toronto Star *building was located at
18–20 King Street West. The main newsroom was
on the third floor while the* Star Weekly *offices that
Hemingway began to haunt were on the second.*
(Toronto Star *photo*)

"What to Do about the Skyscraper Problem," even fretted (complete with diagrams and illustrative arrows) that maybe twenty-story towers would create unnatural wind currents capable of plucking startled Torontonians off the sidewalks and blowing them clear away.

Hemingway climbed the three flights of stairs to the *Star* newsroom, leaning heavily on his walking stick, and entered the newsroom glistening with sweat. Arthur Donaldson greeted him and took him downstairs to the offices of the *Star Weekly*, the *Star*'s weekend feature magazine that offered a mix of inspiring fiction, humorous sketches, comics, children's tales, advice for the love-lorn and pictures of preening peacocks, roaring tigers and water-skiing squirrels.

"Are you busy, boys?" Donaldson asked as he pushed the young man into the cramped office shared by feature editor Greg Clark and cartoonist Jimmy Frise. "This is Ernest Hemingway. He's an American newspaperman. Worked on the *Kansas City Star*. He's up here visiting Ralph Connable."

Greg Clark looked up to see a tall, fresh-faced kid in a peaked hat and leather jacket. He had a noticeable limp. Despite Donaldson's claims that the young man had worked for the *Kansas City Star*, Clark figured he was looking at just another hanger-on. "There is no business in the world in

Star Weekly *features editor Greg Clark did not have*
much faith in the "tall young squirt" who entered
his office one day in January 1920. Although Clark
took Hemingway to be "just another hanger-on" in
the newspaper game, Ernest soon changed
*Clark's mind. (*Toronto Star *photo)*

which there are so many hangers-on as the newspaper business," Clark later wrote. "Eager, hopeful hangers-on. This, I figured, was one of them. He was a large, rather heavy, loose-jointed youth, with a flushed face, dark loose hair and a big red mouth. He perspired easily along his hair on his forehead and under his lower lip."[1]

The cramped space provided just enough room for Clark's desk and typewriter and Frise's drawing board. There was no chair. Hemingway took a seat on the only place you could sit down — on a rusty radiator. "He appeared to be shy, anxious and restless," Clark noted. "He did not have much to say that first afternoon. He just sat on the radiator and answered Jimmie's amiable questions as Jim scratched away at his drawing board. I was busy with my typewriter."

Soon Hemingway was telling stories of his days as a cub reporter in Kansas City. As he listened, Clark continued to believe it highly unlikely that this "tall young squirt had ever written for the Kansas sheet. It was like saying he'd worked for the *Manchester Guardian*." The Kansas City paper was, in those days, "the beau ideal of every newspaperman in America."[2]

Yet Clark did not miss the inference in the way the ad manager had introduced this Hemingway as a guest of Ralph Connable's. Clark figured he and Frise would pretty well have to humor this gangling would-be writer. But that didn't mean they would have to take him seriously. True to Clark's instinct, the big kid hung around all day and did not limp off for the King Street streetcar until the office closed. Clark knew he'd be back.

"Jim," Clark told Frise as they were leaving the office for the evening. "Don't get too chummy with this kid. He'll stick you for ten bucks and that'll be the last of him. He's one of those yearning youngsters, those imaginary guys. *Kansas City Star*, for Pete's sake. Maybe he was an office boy. And Italian Army? Pawff! Him in the Arditi? . . . Probably never was in the war."[3]

Frise replied that Clark had a very suspicious nature.

The *Star Weekly* was a decade old when Hemingway showed up in its offices, and it was beginning to show signs of life after a feeble start. The *Star* and the *Telegram* were the Big Two newspapers that were sniffing and carping at each other in an all-out war for the largest daily circulation in Toronto. But Toronto newsstands also offered three other daily newspapers, the *Globe*, the *Mail and Empire* and the *Toronto World*. (A sixth paper, the *Toronto News*, had folded a year earlier.) Although the *Star* was founded in 1892, the *Star Weekly* was not launched until 1910. It was in-

Toronto had five daily newspapers in 1920. The circulation war was fierce but the Star's *main rival was the* Toronto Telegram. (Toronto Star *photo)*

tended to rival the *Sunday World*, a highly successful feature magazine that would not be easy to knock out of the ring. (Both the *Sunday World* and the *Star Weekly* were actually printed Saturday afternoon to avoid violating Ontario's Lord's Day Act, which prohibited work on Sunday.)

In the *Star Weekly*'s infant years, under editor

J.T. Clark (Greg's father), the magazine ran little else but serious essays, weepy short stories and religious sermons, to reflect the interests of *Star* publisher Joseph "Holy Joe" Atkinson. The early prewar *Weekly* also featured heavy wire-service coverage of news from England, since Toronto was still almost nine-tenths WASP. The pages were filled out with columns by a young Greg Clark and most often revolved around the antics of his infant son. The early *Weekly* operated under a low budget, and circulation grew slowly, for, as one exasperated circulation manager put it, "there was nothing in it but the street cries of London and Greg Clark's baby."[4]

Greg Clark left the *Weekly* to fight in the war, but when he returned was hired as feature editor by the *Weekly*'s new editor, J. Herbert Cranston. Clark soon teamed up with cartoonist Frise to fill the black-and-white pages with colorful puff pieces and cartoons, light stuff for weekend reading, something to distract readers from the raging flu epidemic that was claiming thousands of Torontonians, or the woes of thousands of returned soldiers who still could not find jobs despite putting their lives on the front line for their country during the War to End All Wars. Clark's postwar *Weekly* features alternated between sentimental, homespun fluff, fishing yarns and razzle-dazzle stunt stories. On one scorching summer day, he wrote about frying an egg on the City Hall steps. Another time, he lunged to the sidewalk outside the posh King Edward Hotel and pretended to capture something wild and vicious under his hat. As passersby began to gather, Clark took nervous peeks under the hat, only to slam it down again in feigned terror. Once a hundred or so people had crowded in to watch, Clark merely got up, popped his hat back on his head and went whistling down King Street to whip off a story about the stunt.

The *Star* of this era also employed a promotions manager named Main Johnson (soon to become a close Hemingway friend) who was famous for cooking up bizarre contests to keep up reader interest during slow news periods. In a still-legendary 1912 promotion, the *Star* sponsored a six-week fly-swatting contest for children under sixteen. By the end of the contest, 3,367,680 squashed flies, weighing 2,758 pounds, had been carefully counted and stored in bottles in the Department of Health office. A teen named Beatrice White was crowned the Queen of Swat after personally downing 543,360 flies. For her troubles, White won $50.[5]

By that January day in 1920 when Hemingway met Clark and Frise, the *Star Weekly* had already passed seventy thousand in circulation and, for the first time, was beginning to show a weekly profit of as much as $450. The *Weekly* had its rival, *Sunday World*, staggering on the ropes, but could not seem to land that decisive knock-out punch. In 1920, in an all-out offensive on the *World*'s circulation base, *Star Weekly* editors shifted editorial policy and direction: a picture section would be added, along with short fiction by such popular writers as Ring Lardner, H.G. Wells and Stephen Leacock, for which the *Weekly* paid a princely $100 (although the going rate for freelancers was half a cent a word). But the most radical and significant change was a decision to lighten up the heavy-handed and puritanical tone, to dump the highbrow essays, sermons and didactic fiction in favour of purely entertaining human-interest stories — especially if they could be written with a humorous touch. The object, publisher Atkinson decreed, was not to aim for a sophisticated, posh readership but to go after "the little people in the semi-detached houses."[6] But just exactly where would the *Star Weekly* find a writer with that flare for humor and human interest that could reach this new target audience? The answer was not hard to find.

In fact the answer was impossible to get rid of.

CHAPTER 3

Half a Cent a Word

ERNEST HEMINGWAY BEGAN HAUNTING THE *STAR WEEKLY* OF-fices every day, warming himself on the radiator, telling his tales in his "weird, explosive way of describing things," as Clark remembered it. If even some of his stories were true — and some were, it turned out — this kid had been around. Hemingway, of course, treated his new friends to yet another escalation of his ever evolving tale of his war injury. Fighting shoulder-to-shoulder with the dreaded Arditi regiment, running afoul of explod-ing mortars, dodging — or worse yet, *not* dodging — the hammering machine-gun bullets. Clark would often interject to spin a war story of his own. He had suffered through four years of gruel-ing and costly battles, had won the Military Cross and been promoted to the rank of major during the bloody Canadian victory at Vimy Ridge that saw thousands slaughtered. (The promotion in the field came, the way Clark told his story, "by not getting killed. They could not help making me a major because there was nobody else left.")[1] Cartoonist Jimmy Frise had lost a finger in the fierce battle at Vimy Ridge.

War stories were like fishing stories in those days: everyone told them, but no one quite believed them. And Clark remained especially dubious of Hemingway's war yarns. Sensing this disbelief, Hemingway showed up in Clark's office one day with a small cardboard box. Inside, Clark recalled, were two war medals. One Hemingway had received in a ceremony in Chicago. The other he had been awarded while convalescing in hospital in Milan. Clark, ever the skeptic, checked the medals carefully.

> "Mmmm," I said as I examined them. They were very pretty.
>
> "Itaw-yan," explained Hemmy, without his Ls.
>
> One was the silver cross.
>
> "Croce de Guerra," said Hemmy.
>
> "Ah, like the Military Cross!" I exclaimed.
>
> "This," said Hemmy, a little thickly, showing me a gold one, "is the Medaglia d'Oro per

valore." The highest Italian award, the gold medal for valor.

"Oh, boy!" I automatically turned it on edge. And as long as I live, I shall never forget the cold chill that leaped out, radiating, from my back, and over my shoulders and onto my cheeks. For on the edge was inscribed: "Tenente Ernesto Hemingway." It took me some minutes to get control. Lieut. Ernest Hemingway, who served with the Arditi in the Italian army with great distinction, had been decorated in Chicago by General Diaz.[2]

Clark looked up at the big kid warming himself on the radiator, as if seeing him for the first time. "For Chrissake, Hemingway," he said. "Do you want a job?"

Clark took him in to see J. Herbert Cranston, the *Star Weekly* editor. "Boss," Clark said, "this fellow says he can write, and he wants to do something for us."

Cranston's first impression confirms Clark's description of Ernest, the 1920 edition: Cranston saw "A tall, slim lad with flushed cheeks, glowing black eyes . . . untidy black hair surmounting a round face. He wore a peaked cap, a leather coat short in the arms, and tight, gray trousers that were slightly 'highwater.' He walked with a slight limp."

Cranston questioned Hemingway in a "very matter-of-fact interview." (Although, naturally, few of Ernest's "facts" were wholly based in truth.) Hemingway said he'd "quit school, vagabonded around the United States riding the rods and sleeping in tramp jungles." He told an enthralled Cranston how he'd been forced to live off the land, eating "slugs, snails, earthworms and ants" to survive. He'd done a little work for the *Kansas City Star* but had quit when war broke out. Cranston asked why Hemingway hadn't tried to land a job with a Chicago paper after returning from the war. He'd applied at the *Herald-Examiner*, Hemingway said, but they wouldn't hire him because he "didn't know any policemen."[3] Unlike Clark, Cranston immediately found Hemingway to be a fascinating and credible storyteller. He decided at once to give the young man a chance. Cranston asked Hemingway to go out and find a story and write it up. If it turned out to be any good, the *Weekly* would print it at the usual space rates — half a cent a word.

Hemingway ran out of Cranston's office, shouting to any who would listen that he had "got a job!" He returned to the Connable mansion in an excited state and sat down at his writing desk to compose his first *Star* piece, hammering away at the typewriter in his patented furious flurry.

Star Weekly *editor J.H. Cranston gave Hemingway a*
break after hearing his tall tales of riding the rails
with hoboes and eating slugs and snails to survive.
Cranston offered Hemingway a chance to freelance
for the Weekly *at the going space rate — half a cent*
a word. (Toronto Star *photo)*

"When working on a newspaper assignment," Dorothy Connable recalled, "he typed rapidly until the article was finished — there was no rewriting. . . . He said he never rewrote."[4]

As the target of his first story (see Appendix 1), Hemingway decided to write about Tommy Church, the Toronto mayor who would go on to be elected a record seven times. Hemingway had seen Mayor Church glad-handing with all the returned men at sporting events. Toronto had sent seventy thousand men overseas to fight out of a population of just under half a million. Tommy Church, in his natty suits and signature straw boater always tilted at a jaunty angle, had never failed to see the boys off to the front and never failed to meet a train bringing them back. But ten thousand Toronto men — one in seven who volunteered — died in the war, and thousands more came back with crippling injuries, making Toronto one of the hardest-hit cities, per capita, of any of the allied recruiting centers.

Hemingway felt that any man who had not volunteered was a worthless "slacker." Church was not a young man, but Hemingway felt that age was no excuse: he should have joined the battle. Hemingway had no use for a man who had never seen action or, worse, had not *tried* to see action. And Mayor Church's hobnobbing and joking with the returned soldiers at every public opportunity was more than he could stomach.

Hemingway begins the second paragraph of his finger-pointing profile in arch style:

> From the standpoint of an interested observer, why should an unmarried man of Mayor Church's age, no matter how well exempted, who took no active part in the war, be so popular with the returned men?
>
> Church is undeniably popular with the returned men. Is it because of his military record? You will see a great many men on the streets of Toronto wearing returned buttons who are older than Church. Many of them had wives and families. It was not a young man's war.

He compares the reluctant Mayor Church to an Italian man of similar age whom Hemingway encountered in war-torn Italy.

> I remember in an old school house on the lower Piave River seeing a white haired man seated against the wall looking glumly at the blood-soaked emergency dressing that covered the shattered stump at his wrist.
>
> While we were waiting for our turn at the

table I spoke to him. He was a volunteer. His home was in Abruzzi. He would be fifty-five years old next month. He grunted his answers and looked at the wall.

"You're too old, Dad, for this war," I said. He resented that. The glum look left his face. He sneered. That sneer included me, my youth, all illusions and war itself.

"Corpo di Bacco!" he snapped "I can die as well as any man."[5]

Hemingway submitted his story to the *Star Weekly*, yet although it showed flashes of promise, the editors apparently felt the attack on Church was too ham-handed. To Hemingway's disgust, the piece was rejected. First the *Saturday Evening Post* and now even the *Star Weekly* were refusing his material. He returned to the Connable home visibly discouraged, tossing the rejected manuscript to Dorothy Connable. He wanted no more part of it.

During the evenings, Hemingway tried to fulfill his "paid companion" obligations by taking Junior to sporting events such as the National Hockey League games at Mutual Street Arena. The Toronto St. Pats were not a great team in 1920. They had finished dead-last the year before but were now rebuilding, heading for a .500 season and third place behind the powerhouse Ottawa Senators and the Montreal Maroons. To Hemingway's delight, the mediocre Toronto team had the toughest players in the league, bent on proving they could beat their opponents in the alley, if not on the scoreboard. The games were hard-hitting, frequently erupting into bloody brawls. Ernest enjoyed himself immensely, even if young Ralph clearly cringed from the violence.[6]

Then as now, all of Toronto was crazy about hockey. Hemingway began teaching himself to skate on the Connables' backyard rink. He would rise at dawn (he still could not sleep very well, an insomniac ever since his wounding), to strap on skates "as dull as your ordinary kitchen knife." He would wobble around the rink, soon learning to glide if not to actually stop or turn. As much as it hurt, it helped his injured leg and knee grow slowly stronger.

Even as a young man, Hemingway clearly did not like to lose and he did not like to be second-best at anything. He had to be the best fisherman, the best shot, the best boxer, the best drinker, the best writer. He viewed any sport, even a hike or a swim, as a chance to show up his rivals, even if his "rivals" were not aware that it was a contest. To the end of his days he compared himself to other writers — living and dead — in sporting terms. Sports, like bullfighting or boxing, allowed Hemingway to see how men reacted under pressure. And "grace under pressure" became one of the most important themes in his later fiction.

Hemingway soon joined hockey games against players of much greater skill, including Ernest Smith, a star on the University of Toronto team. Smith and other players quickly learned that, even though Hemingway couldn't exactly skate, it was wise to keep one's head up when he was on the ice. What Hemingway lacked in talent he made up for in enthusiasm. He would line up an opposing player for a bodycheck and take a long, wobbly run at him. "All you had to do was sidestep him," Smith said, "and he couldn't stop. He'd go headfirst right for the snow bank." But then he would always pick himself up, take aim on a new target and — like a charging bull — repeat the process. Smith and Hemingway soon became good friends.[7]

One day, a young Englishman, a guest of a Connable neighbor, dropped by the rink to look down his nose at the hockey game in progress. As Dorothy Connable remembered it, the Englishman yawned that he was amazed by Canadians' ignorance of the "sports and sportsmanship they are always talking about." He said he had "failed to find either in Canada." This was clearly the wrong thing to say in the company of a houseguest like Ernest Hemingway.

"Ernest, who enjoyed dramatic situations, suggested they give the man who had insulted Canada a working over," Dorothy recalled. Hemingway challenged the Englishman to a skating competition. The snob was, by some small miracle, a worse skater than Hemingway and was soon limping to the bench on overturned ankles. "Tired?" Hemingway asked, feigning surprise. "Are you stopping?" Although his war injury made it painful for him to totter around on blades he could barely stand on himself, Hemingway forced his victim to keep on skating, refusing him a chance to rest. It was almost midnight when Hemingway broke off the skating. The Englishman slumped on the bench, gasping, red-faced. "How about skiing down the ravine?" Hemingway asked him. "Or trying the rowing machine?" When the wheezing opponent weakly waved off both invitations, Hemingway suggested it was time to go upstairs and try on the boxing gloves. The British braggart turned and stumbled off into the night, fleeing for home, explaining feebly that it was "an odd hour for boxing."[8] There was no need for gloves. Hemingway knew he had scored his knockout.

CHAPTER 4

The Sum Also Rises

HEMINGWAY'S FIRST STORY, THE RATHER HARSH ATTACK ON the mayor, was not published. But soon afterward he was producing articles and features that the *Star* and the *Star Weekly* saw fit to print. All other Hemingway biographies and bibliographies, including *Dateline, Toronto: The Complete Toronto Star Dispatches*, maintain that Hemingway's first story to be published by the *Toronto Star* appeared on February 14, 1920: a short, unsigned *Star Weekly* piece headlined "Circulating Pictures a New High-Art Idea in Toronto." This sarcasm-dipped report blows the whistle on a scheme by Toronto housewives to rent paintings from prominent artists during the summer social whirl, presumably to dupe their party guests into thinking they were matrons of wealth and taste.

The official record indicates that it was three more weeks before Hemingway's second *Star Weekly* piece was printed — the first to appear under his byline. This second story, published March 6 under the headline "Taking a Chance for a Free Shave," again shows Hemingway's talent for making a human-interest yarn out of just about anything. The story begins in vintage early Hemingway style — assured, humorous and anything but terse (he was, after all, being paid by the word): "The land of the free and the home of the brave is the modest phrase used by certain citizens to the south of us to designate the country they live in. They may be brave — but nothing is free. Free lunch passed some time ago and on attempting to join the Freemasons you are informed it will cost you seventy-five dollars."

There is no doubt that Hemingway wrote both these early pieces. (He was so proud of the "Free Shave" yarn that he carried the clipping in his wallet for months to come.) But there is strong reason to believe that these stories were not Hemingway's earliest *Star* efforts, but rather his fifth and sixth submissions to the paper. That was the belief of former *Toronto Star* librarian William McGeary.

McGeary was a *Star* reporter when Hemingway joined the paper. However, years later, in 1935 a

tragic and accidental death in his family so shattered him that he was taken off reporting duties
and reassigned to work in the *Star* library. There
he immersed himself in meticulous research. For
the last twenty-five years of his life — he died
in 1984 at ninety-one — McGeary investigated Hemingway's Toronto period, identifying stories for
Carlos Baker's biography, *Ernest Hemingway: A Life
Story*. Even after Baker's biography was published
in 1969 he continued to identify Hemingway stories, so that when I began my research, I found
nine volumes of yellowing papers that made up
McGeary's work on Hemingway in the *Star* archives. Included in his files were typescripts of
all the Hemingway stories he identified for Baker.
(Stories verified by McGeary also make up 158
of the 172 pieces in *Dateline, Toronto*.) But in addition to the known stories were typescripts of five
uncollected stories McGeary firmly believed Hemingway had written. McGeary's supporting evidence and the familiar style of these five articles
make a convincing case.

The first is an unsigned story headlined "New
Ether to Credit of Toronto Surgeon," which ap-
peared in the *Daily Star* of January 27, 1920. A
week later, an unsigned follow-up piece ran in the
Star Weekly titled "Truth-telling Ether a Secret."
(See Appendices 2 and 3.) Both works are ob-

William McGeary, the late Toronto Star *librarian,
made a life work of researching Hemingway's
Toronto days. He not only identified 158 of the 172
stories included in the "complete" Toronto record
contained in* Dateline, Toronto, *but also five more
stories that appear for the first time in this book.*
(Toronto Star *photo)*

viously based on the same interview and both er-
roneously refer to the Canadian Medical Association as the "Dominion Association," an outdated
title a Canadian reporter would never use. A To-
rontonian would also never refer to the University
of Toronto as "Toronto University," as this reporter
does (and as Hemingway did in another verified
Star Weekly story). Also, the writer mistakes the
dean of medicine at the U. of T. for the dean of
the entire university. All of these details indicate
not only that the same reporter wrote both pieces
but also that the reporter was new to the city and
probably new to the country, as was Hemingway.

The first story, "New Ether," is a straight news
piece of the sort Hemingway used to churn out
while covering the hospital beat for the *Kansas City
Star*. But the second story, "Truth-telling Ether a
Secret," features a whimsical lead that rings of Hemingway's other early humorous human-interest
features for the *Weekly*. It also displays Hemingway's idiosyncratic handling of "that" and
"which":

> Unfortunately for jealous wives, detectives and
> truth seekers in general, Dr. James H. Cotton's
> new ether . . . does not make the patient tell
> the truth, the whole truth and nothing but the
> truth.

During Dr. Cotton's research work, an ether combination was discovered which did that very thing. And Dr. Cotton could supply governments, if it were considered in the interest of humanity, with that secret formula. No doubt, private enterprises will immediately set to work experimenting on that other miraculous ether, and we will see cunning advertisements of "Veracity Ether, recommended to suspicious wives, detectives, politicians, etc." For during these experiments in 1916 and 1917, Dr. Cotton was constrained to stop some of his subjects from telling the unvarnished stories of their lives.

Both Hemingway's sister Marcelline and brother, Leicester, later remembered that Hemingway had written home to say his first *Star* assignment had been to interview a doctor. Marcelline recalls in her memoir *At the Hemingways*: "It seems [Ernest] was sent by the *Star* to interview a man famous in the medical world. When the copy was finished, Ernest was complimented by the editor on getting all the correct technical facts and the exact medical phraseology. When Dad heard this, he was pleased but not surprised. He said it showed Ernest's good training as a doctor's son."[1] Yet no doctor stories appear among his known early works collected in

Dateline, Toronto. If the ether stories are indeed by Hemingway, they represent his first two contributions to the *Toronto Star.*

Another McGeary find is "Red Flag in Toronto" (February 14, 1920), an unsigned short story about a Bolshevik hobo who had "recently arrived from Chicago." (See Appendix 4.) At the time the story appeared, Hemingway had, of course, also recently arrived from a Chicago where communists were being rounded up in raids. "Red Flag in Toronto" is shot through with hobo slang, such as an "armful of rods," the same phrase that editor Cranston remembers Hemingway using during his first *Star Weekly* interview. When working for the *Kansas City Star,* Hemingway would often hang out in the rail yards with the hoboes, and prided himself on learning their jargon.

Other circumstantial evidence indicates that Hemingway wrote "Red Flag in Toronto." While living with the Connables, he went home from the *Star* up Bathurst Street, as does the protagonist of "Red Flag." Hemingway also enjoyed wandering along Queen Street West, where two of his other early verified stories are set. These two streets figure prominently in "Red Flag in Toronto":

A rather dazed and weary Sam walked up Bathurst Street to Queen. He had a few Yankee coins in his pocket. For, while being a Red was a pleasant and thrilling occupation, it was not lucrative, yet. . . .

Sam had only seen the Red Flag in the secrecy of the dimmest and deepest cellars in Chicago, where only the boldest of the Reds were assembled.

In this article — really more like a rather juvenile short story — Hemingway writes in short sentences and displays a thinly veiled sarcasm. Once in Toronto, the Red walks "up-town," as only a Chicago native would write. The Red, who speaks no English, sees a red flag and enters what he thinks is a communist meeting, not realizing it is an auction in progress:

> That decided it. Canada had had the revolution, and Sam hadn't heard of it while in hiding! That was it. The Red flag had come, and the workers were supreme! . . . The Speaker was making a very Red speech, by the sound of it.

Greg Clark was the only other *Star* reporter on the *Weekly* staff in 1920 who was known for writing this type of light and obviously apocryphal piece. But Clark, a columnist, surely would have been given a byline. Years later, McGeary showed "Red Flag" to Clark, who replied in a letter: "This is definitely not mine and I am fairly in agreement with you that it was Hemingway. . . . Yes, I would vote for this being Hemmy and perhaps his first or one of his first essays on breaking into the *Weekly.*"[2]

Modern newspapers slap bylines on every six-inch ambulance-chasing report that comes out of the general-assignment or summer-student pool. In 1920, however, a byline was an uncommon reward and not usually granted until a writer had earned it with exceptional unsigned work. (Gordon Sinclair, who went on to become a well-known writer and broadcaster, wrote for the *Star* for more than seven years in the 1920s before he received his first byline.) And yet *Dateline, Toronto* shows that Hemingway earned a byline for his second known piece — an unlikely feat for an unproven twenty-year-old. Jimmy Cowan, who served as an editor on the *Star Weekly* in 1920, remembered that Hemingway's "early stuff went into the [*Weekly*] news section and wasn't by-lined."[3] All the evidence therefore suggests that Hemingway's first byline came on his fifth *Star* feature, not his second as biographies and bibliographies state.

"The *Star Weekly*," editor J.H. Cranston later recalled, "aimed to give the people largely what they wanted to read rather than what they ought to read if they were to become intelligent citizens."[4] And Ernest Hemingway soon proved that he was able to deliver such stories in spades. Along with his entertaining "Circulating Art" and "Free Shave" stories, he offered expert primers on how to do outdoorsy things like camping, fishing and canoeing. Humor and a sense of omniscience are the most impressive traits of Hemingway's early *Toronto Star* stories. "Hemingway," Cranston was soon convinced, "could write in good, plain Anglo-Saxon, and had a certain much prized gift of humor."[5] The *Star Weekly* staff soon began to realize that they had found just the right young writer to reach that reader in the semi-detached house that publisher Joseph Atkinson had targeted.

The *Toronto Star* was nothing like the other *Star* in Kansas City on which Hemingway served an eight-month apprenticeship in 1917. As a cub reporter in Kansas City, Hemingway had the basics of routine journalism drilled into his head while crafting short who-what-why-when-and-where stories about the doings at the hospital, train station and police headquarters. He never received a byline, and nothing distinctive is evident in any of the unsigned Kansas City pieces that have been attributed to him. The eighteen-year-old filed his work to editors who incessantly rewrote and heavily tampered with his copy. Forced to adhere to the Kansas City *Star* style sheet, he was given no freedom to choose his subjects or practice anything that could be called creative writing. Most of his stories were phoned in to more experienced rewrite men, who crafted the facts to fit the newspaper's mold.

In Toronto, however, the editors tended to leave it up to the reporters to suggest ideas and to set the tone and style for their features. In this way, the newspaper soon became a testing ground for the young Hemingway. The *Star* had no rewrite men, and the editors were ordered to go light with the pencil. "I don't like a newspaper that seems to have been all run out of one mold," said publisher Atkinson, who felt that rewriting or heavy editing robbed a story of its freshness and its appeal for the little people.[6] If a reporter showed a distinctive style — as Hemingway quickly did — this was the surest ticket to rapid advancement. As long as it was light-hearted, a humorous and flippant tone was encouraged. Take, for example, the closing paragraphs of Hemingway's "Free Shave" piece: "If you wish to secure free board, free room and free medical attention, there is one infallible way of obtaining it. Walk up to the biggest policeman you can find and hit him in the face.

Toronto Star *publisher Joseph "Holy Joe" Atkinson*
admired reporters who had a distinctive style and a
sense of humor. The freedom of expression he
ordered his editors to permit allowed Hemingway a
chance to write articles that had more to do with
*fiction than journalism. (*Toronto Star *photo)*

The length of your period of free board and room
will depend on how [police magistrate] Colonel
Denison is feeling. And the amount of your free

medical attention will depend on the size of the policeman."

Encouraged by the enthusiastic acceptance of his "Free Shave" story, Hemingway decided to take another shot at the glad-handing Mayor Tommy Church.

This time, he shows more subtlety and wit. His touch is lighter but his words still cut with a knife. The article deftly lampoons Church's attempts to portray himself as an ardent sports fan, only to be betrayed by his absolute ignorance of boxing while pressing the flesh at a bout at Massey Hall:

> It looked as though the mayor enjoyed the last bout best of all. Of course, he didn't see it, but he discovered several people he had not shaken hands with, and there was a great deal of booing and cheering. Sometimes the mayor would absentmindedly boo when the crowd cheered but he always righted himself instinctively at once. He seemed able to shift a boo into a cheer with the same ease and grace of shoving a Ford into low gear. . . . The mayor is just as interested in hockey as boxing. If cootie fighting or Swedish pinochle or Australian boomerang hurling are ever taken up by the voters, count on the mayor to be there in a ringside seat. For the mayor loves all sports.

"Sporting Mayor" was published in the *Star Weekly* of March 13, 1920. "It was good," Greg Clark said of the piece years later. "Maybe we didn't know how good."[7] It was only Hemingway's second byline, but already the *Star*'s editors were beginning to take serious notice of this young kid from the States.

Hemingway would later dismiss his journalism as work that he dashed off for strictly mercenary reasons. But there is no doubt — at least early on — that he took his newspaper writing more seriously than this. On one occasion, he showed a *Star Weekly* story in progress to Dorothy Connable, ostensibly asking for advice but no doubt fishing for praise. When Dorothy offered some criticism and suggested ways to improve the story, Hemingway showed a side she'd never seen — he became angry and then fell into a moody depression. Dorothy was surprised by how her "criticism troubled him."[8] She wisely decided to never again offer any comment on Ernest's fledgling newspaper work.

From very early on, Hemingway clipped his *Star* articles and mailed them to his parents and friends. And, at this stage in his writing career at least, the reviews from home were positive. Seeing at last some black-and-white proof of Hemingway's claim that he could break into print, his mother and father sent words of praise and encouragement. "The Free Shave story etc. was very good indeed," Clarence wrote his son proudly. "I am sure you will succeed."[9]

CHAPTER 5

Booze, Bass and Boxing

ALTHOUGH HEMINGWAY HAD ALREADY DECIDED THAT RALPH Junior was no fun, being left alone with a free run of the Connable mansion did offer its compensations. He had already developed a keen taste for hard liquor during his war days, and for a kid from Prohibition-dry Chicago, the Connable house was like the proverbial candy store. Only a year earlier, Canadians had also been prohibited from buying alcohol except for "medicinal" reasons. But even then, to get a bottle in Ontario, as Stephen Leacock recorded, one had merely "to go to the drugstore . . . and lean up against the counter and make a gurgling sound like apoplexy. One often sees these apoplexy cases lined up four deep."[1] Indeed, one Toronto doctor wrote 487 prescriptions for medicinal spirits in one eight-hour day — or one prescription per minute.

By 1920, under pressure from returned men and the more liberal voters from Quebec, the Canadian temperance laws were relaxed. Although it was still illegal to sell alcohol in public bars, it was now legal to produce it, buy it by mail-order and possess it for use in private dwellings. As a frequent host, Mr. Connable kept an ample supply of booze in his Lyndhurst Avenue basement, stored in a huge vault designed to prevent rum-running "hooch gangs" from breaking in and plundering the supply for sale across the lake in the United States. Though this may sound far-fetched and paranoid, a hooch gang did raid the Connable home in 1923, foiled only after a shootout with police.

Hemingway's Toronto friends recalled his strong resentment of Prohibition — and his keen interest in the contents of Mr. Connable's liquor vault. He was careful not to be seen drinking while Mr. and Mrs. Connable were around, and even Dorothy recalled that they drank only fine wines in the house, and then only on state occasions. But other friends remember that once the Connables headed south, Ernest dipped into the liquor vault freely. Ernest Smith, the varsity hockey star whom Hemingway had futilely charged on the rink, became a drinking companion of Hemingway's while the family was away. The cellar, Smith recalled, "was enough to turn a bootlegger green with envy. All authentic stuff — the family never touched it. It was only when people came in."

Even before the teetotalling family headed south, Hemingway was known to sneak a few bottles. Smith, who was as good with a billiards cue as he was with a hockey stick, remembered a snooker match that Hemingway had set up in the Connable house between Smith and another local shark, Bert Cowan. Smith arrived for the game, only to be intercepted by Hemingway: "The family were there and some other people," Smith said, "I was met by Hemmy and he said, 'I've got five dollars on you.' He said we'd better prepare. So we went into the dining room to the sideboard and he poured me two drinks. I'd swear they were that big [holding up four fingers]. And [he had] a couple himself and showed me the five dollars he was putting on me. . . . And when I got to the table I couldn't tell the white bone from the red bone."[2]

Smith lost the game badly. But Hemingway's money was safe. It turned out he had actually bet his five dollars on Bert Cowan.

When Ernest Hemingway first came to perch on the radiator in the *Star Weekly* office, he promptly made sure that everyone knew he was expert in hunting, fishing, camping and canoeing. He told wild tales of his adventures, exaggerating his fish stories to the same degree that he pumped up his war exploits. Like any good freelancer, Hemingway was adept at turning his anecdotes and yarns into fast (if rather paltry) cash, penning half a dozen *Star Weekly* features that let middle-class city folks live his adventures vicariously.

Feature editor Greg Clark, a noted outdoorsman himself who later wrote many books about fishing, was initially just as doubtful of Hemingway's fish stories as he was about his war or newspaper yarns — or anything else that came out of the young man's mouth. Nobody, especially not one so young, could have done so much, so well. One day Clark decided to call Hemingway's bluff and invited him to go fishing on the Credit River, about forty miles north of Toronto.

Hemingway showed up with an eight-ounce rod that had to be ten feet long. This ungainly gear confirmed to Clark that Hemingway was a clumsy, ill-equipped neophyte, that his fish stories were a "bit of a fraud, just like the *Kansas City Star* stuff." But once they got their lines in the water, Hemingway quickly bagged trout after trout with his graceful and accurate casting and his knowledge of the quarry. "By golly, he was a first-class fly fisherman," Clark had to admit to himself. "With this very unwieldy tackle, he got more trout than I did."[3] Clark was slowly learning that perhaps there was something to this "tall young squirt" after all.

Although Hemingway did not write any fiction about his Toronto days, he clearly used his *Star Weekly* features as the basis for a number of his short stories. His April 24, 1920, piece titled "Trout-Fishing Hints" was the direct model for his famous short story "Big Two-Hearted River." In "Trout-Fishing Hints," Hemingway writes:

> The big difficulty about fishing with grasshoppers has always been the difficulty in catching them. The classic way is to get up early in the morning before the sun has dried the dew and catch the hoppers while they are still stiff and cold and unable to hop more than a feeble foot or two. They are found under the side of logs in a clearing and along the grass stems.

A similar passage employing the less explanatory and more figurative language of fiction appears in "Big Two-Hearted River."

The meadow was wet with dew and Nick wanted to catch grasshoppers for bait before the sun dried the grass. He found plenty of good grasshoppers. They were at the base of the grass stems. Sometimes they clung to the grass stems. They were cold and wet with the dew and could not jump until the sun warmed them. Nick picked them up, taking only the medium-sized ones, and put them into the bottle. He turned over a log and just under the shelter of the edge were several hundred hoppers. It was a grasshopper lodging house.[4]

There are dozens of such parallels in basic style, subject and tone between Hemingway's *Star* features and short stories. Elsewhere in the same trout-fishing primer, Hemingway describes how to put a grasshopper on a hook: "Put the hook in under the chin of the grasshopper and carry it back through the thorax." In "Big Two-Hearted River," Nick Adams puts his advice to practical use: "Nick took [the grasshopper] by the head and held him until he threaded the slim hook under his chin, down through his thorax and into the last segments of his abdomen."

Hemingway wrote so many of these outdoorsy how-to stories that it seems he created a glut for the editors of the *Weekly*. That would explain, according to the long-moldering files of the *Star*'s William McGeary, why another such wilderness-tip feature was held until the summer of 1922, published unsigned and never before identified as the work of Hemingway. The lost story (see Appendix 9) was headlined "Before You Go on a Canoe Trip, Learn Canoeing." This sparely written and still-informative primer on canoeing uses a style similar to known Hemingway *Star* features on camping and fishing. All of these are written in the assured voice of a consummate expert, a matter-of-absolute-fact voice Hemingway would use in sporting stories for the rest of his life: "Weed out something from your kit every time you look at it in preparation. Go easy on the clothes. You will sleep in them anyway, most likely, and you must wash linen as you go. Wash at night and dry by the camp fire."[5]

Here is such trademark free expert advice delivered in similar style in Hemingway's verified *Star* story "Trout-Fishing Hints": "Worms, grubs, beetles, crickets and grasshoppers are some of the best trout baits. But worms and hoppers are the most widely used. . . . Watch the line at the tip of your pole. As soon as it straightens out the least bit, strike with your wrist. Don't wait for the jerk before striking."

A famous trait in Hemingway's fiction style is his preoccupation with minutely detailing the preparation and consummation of food (and later, beverages). In "Before You Go on a Canoe Trip, Learn Canoeing," he demonstrates this short, recipe-book style as he offers, in clipped lists similar to the previous verified passage, what food should be brought along: "A side of bacon, cakes of dried soup, butter in a tin, jam in a tin, tea and sugar in small salt bags, condensed milk if you must have milk, then cans of beans, meat, etc. A box of patent pancake flour is a good thing. Empty it into a tin. Take no glass."

The style and cadence are echoed in the known Hemingway *Star* story called "When You Camp Out, Do It Right" (June 26, 1920): "With the prepared pancake flour you take a cupful of pancake flour and add a cup of water. Mix the water and flour and as soon as the lumps are out it is ready for cooking. Have a skillet hot and keep it well greased. Apple butter, syrup or cinnamon and sugar go well with the cakes."

In turn, a passage that echoes both of the known *Star Weekly* stories occurs in "Big Two-Hearted River": "Rapidly he mixed some buckwheat flour with water and stirred it smooth, one cup of flour, one cup of water. He put a handful of coffee in the pot and dipped a lump of grease out of a can

Dear Bill

This is definitely not mine, and I am fairly in agreement with you that it was Hemingway.

Yes, I would vote for this being Hemmy and perhaps his first or one of his first essays at breaking into the Weekly. he hun_ around Jimmie's and my room every day, and for a fairly long time before I took him into Cranston — "Here's a young fellow wants to write for us."

— Greg Clark x

Greg Clark confirmed the authenticity of McGeary's uncollected find "Before You Go on a Canoe Trip, Learn Canoeing" with this letter written on May 28, 1965.

(Toronto Star Archives)

and slid it sputtering across the hot skillet. On the smoking skillet he poured smoothly the buckwheat batter. . . . Nick ate a big flapjack and a smaller one, covered with apple butter."[6]

Hemingway and Greg Clark were the only two outdoorsmen writing for the *Weekly* in the early 1920s, and in a letter to McGeary, Clark confirmed that he did not write "Before You Go on a Canoe Trip, Learn Canoeing." Clark agreed that this had to be the unrecognized work of the young Ernest Hemingway.

With the Connables away in Florida, Hemingway did his best to hold up his end of the bargain in trying to convert young Ralph into a manly specimen. Ernest and his Petoskey pal Dutch Pailthrop introduced Ralph to boxing during a particularly messy match at Massey Hall between Fern Bull and Rocky Kansas. Ernest watched the gory fight with obvious glee and pointed out the finer points. But Ralph was only sickened by the spurting blood.

When not writing his human-interest pieces for the *Star* or dragging Ralph Junior to assorted blood sports around town, Hemingway still clung to his dream of becoming a fiction writer. He continued to write short stories, which, like his early journalism, were written in the voice of the know-it-all public lecturer. He also read everything he could find in bookstores and the Connables' well-stocked library. He took particular interest in Havelock Ellis's *Erotic Symbolism*, which described numerous rather acrobatic positions for sexual intercourse, and was especially fascinated with the section on sexual fetishes, which included several twists on desire fired by cross-sexual haircuts — men with women's hair, women with men's hair — an obsession that would resurface in his unpublished fragments and in the posthumous novel, *The Garden of Eden*. Hemingway sent a copy of *Erotic Symbolism* to his friend Bill Smith to prove, as the book declared and as Hemingway always contended in campfire man-talk, that women enjoyed sex as much as men — a rather shocking notion in 1920.

The Connable library gave Hemingway his first taste of the works of Joseph Conrad, a writer who would influence his own later work. By April, he was enthusiastically recommending Conrad's *Victory* in a letter to his ambulance service friend Ted Brumback, who agreed that Conrad was "the king of them all." Under Conrad's spell, Hemingway and Brumback began planning a sea journey of their own, to ship out to the Orient on a tramp steamer in the fall.

Hemingway still held out high hopes for short stories he had written the previous summer up in Michigan. A month before arriving in Toronto, he had written to Bill Smith to report that the *Saturday Evening Post* had rejected yet another story (unappetizingly named "Wolves and Doughnuts"). But the editor of *Popular Magazine* had not yet turned down another story with the equally unpromising name "The Woppian Way" (a bad pun on the Appian Way, the famed ancient road out of Rome). "Hope to God he may buy it," Hemingway told Smith. "Non hearage from him is a good sign at any rate. A better sign would be a large check."

"The Woppian Way" featured an appearance by Hemingway's hero, Gabriele D'Annunzio, who is described in the story as "the great amourist who had exhausted the love of women and now was wringing the last drops of love of country into his white hot soul." Another of Hemingway's short stories of this period, "The Mercenaries," again refers to D'Annunzio, this time in a duel with a young soldier (not unlike Ernest) over a woman with "blue-black hair and a face colored like old ivory and eyes like inkwells and full red lips." In retrospect, it is easy to see why the stories Hemingway toiled over in his early months in Toronto were so aggressively rejected.

The previous summer, Hemingway had shown "The Woppian Way" to an older writer named Edwin Balmer, who had a cottage near the Hemingway summer place. Balmer told him that the stories showed promise; his most useful suggestion was to remove the sledgehammer racism of the title "The Woppian Way" by changing it to "The Passing of Pickles McCarthy." Thus encouraged, Hemingway now hoped that this published writer would act as his agent and help him break into print. He sent some new stories to Balmer's home, listing potential markets but adding that he would leave it to the more experienced writer where to sell the stories and how much to charge. Balmer's response arrived in the Connable mailbox early in February. He said that one or two of the stories might be salable, "but not necessarily immediately salable. The list you have mentioned is really no sort of try-out." Balmer then tried to soften the blow of likely rejection: "Perhaps I will be able to do no more than to find out what is the editorial objection to the stories, but I'll get that, at least. The funny feature of the writing business is that you simply can not tell what will go; I've seen things in print that I wouldn't believe anyone could possibly buy; and I've seen things turned down that I couldn't see how anyone could pass up. But those do remain forever turned down."[7]

In February of 1920, Harriet Connable wrote to tell Hemingway the news from Palm Beach. Among other chit-chat, she related a story about how Dorothy had gone to a casino with five dollars and returned with seventeen dollars' profit and a great new interest in roulette. Sensing a new opportunity to impress with his expertise, Hemingway rushed off a long letter to Dorothy explaining that he felt it was his duty to stop work on his magnum opus, "Night Life of the European Capitals, Or The War as I Seen It," to offer — in great detail and complete with diagrams — a treatise on his own sure-fire system to beat the roulette wheel consistently, a system "worked out by bitter experience in the very best gambling halls of Yarrup." In keeping with his already kindled belief in living within a code of honor, Hemingway added a note about ethics among gamblers: "Probably you aren't really interested in roulette any way. But it is the best game in the world, having the advantage over craps that in craps you are winning your friend's money and consequently it is not so much fun. But in roulette you are bucking a wheel and there are no ethics against quitting when you are ahead. You can't do that in craps or poker. It is the loser who has to say when to quit. But in roulette when you get a decent way ahead — quit."[8]

Ernest Hemingway made a life work of taking chances, and even as a twenty-year-old, he already saw himself as an expert in gambling. He soon became close friends with cartoonist Jimmy Frise, who welcomed his visits to the *Weekly* offices as a handy excuse to procrastinate from the task of drawing his cartoons. Frise was famous for producing nothing on paper all week and then staying up all night to meet the 2 p.m. Saturday press deadline with only seconds to spare. Not only did the unaffected and unassuming Frise love to gossip but he also loved to gamble, and would frequently slip away early to put money on a "sure thing" at Woodbine racetrack or try his notoriously bad luck with the dice in crap games. In Hemingway, he found a willing conspirator.

Although most of Hemingway's *Star Weekly* pieces concerned outdoor sports, he also made it plain that he considered himself an authority on what he euphemistically referred to as "indoor sports." In a May 1920 piece about crap-shooting headlined "Galloping Dominoes, Alias African Golf, Taken Up by Toronto's Smart Set," Hemingway explained the rudiments of rolling the "joy cubes" in "Louisiana Lacrosse," then added a note of warning for anyone who might think a mere novice could master the game: "Craps is only to a limited extent a game of chance. If you don't believe this, try your luck against an experienced manipulator of the ivories. It shouldn't take him any longer than about six passes to convince you that craps is a game of skill."

Hemingway was adept at just about any sport you could name (with the exception of ice hockey), yet he considered boxing his special talent. He had already developed his odd habit of shadowboxing during conversations or while walking along the street. He was only too happy to advise much older *Star* colleagues such as Main Johnson on how to dress like an insider when going to boxing matches. (Hemingway told Johnson never to go to the arena in "citified" clothes, but to wear a red pullover and a cap pulled down over one eye.)

The *Star* already employed legendary sports writer Lou Marsh on the boxing beat, so the only way that Hemingway could show his ring knowledge in print was to devise articles with feature or opinion angles. The Tommy Church "Sporting Mayor" article gave him a chance to describe the fights at Massey Hall from an insider's perspective. In May of 1920, Hemingway got back into the ring by taking the slant that, for the first time, women were allowed to attend a Toronto boxing match, this time an exhibition bout by one of Hemingway's heroes, French heavyweight champ Georges Carpentier, who was soon to fight world heavyweight champion Jack Dempsey. By June of 1921, as the Dempsey–Carpentier fight grew near, Hemingway had ended his first visit to Toronto but mailed two stories to the *Star* from Chicago, in which he handicapped the big bout. But, as Clark replied in a letter misdated June 25, 1920 (it was actually 1921), managing editor John Bone could not place the stories. "He explained to me how fully we were covering the fight from every angle," Clark wrote, "two or three news services, Ring Lardner, a couple of special writers and our own sporting staff." Sports editor Bill Hewitt also declared the stories "O.K." but told Clark they "hardly fitted in with what we were publishing . . . and we already contracted for more copy than we could print." As it turned out, Clark managed to place the first story in the most unlikely spot: the feature position on the *Star*'s editorial page. With the enclosed clipping, Clark added, "Oh enviable Hemmy of the edit page — an honor I have obtained but *once!*"[9] Although bylined, this story has been overlooked — perhaps because of its unusual placement in the newspaper and because Clark's letter was misdated by one year. It is not included in the *Dateline, Toronto* collection. The other story, "What Professional Boxers Fight For," was rejected.

Hemingway considered himself an expert on the sport of boxing, both as a participant and an analyst, and his handicapping of the talents of then-heavyweight champion Jack Dempsey was published in the Toronto Star's *editorial page.*
(Toronto Star *Archives*)

Both appear here for the first time as Appendices 5 and 6.

In "The Superman Myth," Hemingway maintains that world champ Jack Dempsey's reputation is undeserved because he did not face a tough opponent on the way to the title. Hemingway gives a blow-by-blow account of the July 4, 1919, fight in which Dempsey won the championship from a boozy, over-the-hill boxer named Jess Willard:

On July 4th, 40 years old, heavy, paunched, untrained and sodden and loggy with two years of steady drinking, [Willard] went forth with cow-like courage to fight Jack Dempsey for the championship of the world and $150,000 win, lose or draw. In the first round, the slim, sun-browned Dempsey slugged him to the canvas seven times. Willard looked dumbly and stupidly up at the tiger-like youth and staggered to his feet to earn this $150,000. At the end of the third round Dempsey was tired from smashing the big bulk and Willard seemed to be recuperating from the beating he had taken. Willard seemed the fresher of the two — Dempsey was hanging on to him and occasionally socking in a tired manner.

Willard's seconds tossed in the towel at the start of the fourth round. Jess believed he had given the fans a run for their admission — and he didn't need the championship any more — he had $150,000.

Hemingway went on to predict that European champion Carpentier would annihilate the pretender Dempsey in the coming 1921 battle, quoting a Toronto pug named Harry Greb who said, "The Frenchman is lucky — any good fast man, who can hit, will take Jack Dempsey. I envy Carpentier his chance." So sure was Hemingway of the outcome of this title fight that he not only put his reputation as an expert on the line but also wagered $50 on Carpentier.

Dempsey knocked out Carpentier in the fourth round.

CHAPTER 6

A Ghostwriter Abroad,
1921

HEMINGWAY'S JOB AS PAID COMPANION AT THE CONNABLE home officially ended in May of 1920, after the family returned from Florida. But he stayed on for a month afterwards. He would often stop by Harriet Connable's writing desk as she prepared her reports for her various charitable societies and compare writing styles, wondering aloud why her sentences were so long when his were so short. In a note after departing, he told Mrs. Connable "how much [he] enjoyed and appreciated being in [her] home. You were awfully good to me and I want you to know how much it meant to me to know you all, in addition to the priceless time I had." He then added that he looked forward to seeing the Connables up in Michigan cottage country over the coming summer. "I've told my family many times that you are the very nicest people I've ever known and I look forward to having them meet you so they will agree with me."[1]

Although Hemingway genuinely liked most of the Connables, he was relieved to be rid of his duties in trying to mold and shape the character of Ralph Junior, whom he would later describe as "a good kid but fairly twisted up and he was that type that is stupid in his studies to the point almost of idiocy yet very crafty in bringing out very intelligent remarks. You could not train him to box, but I saw that he got exercise and kept him out of trouble. But I knew any job of mine with him was hopeless."[2]

By June Hemingway was back up in cottage country, and from there he began bombarding the *Star* with feature stories on everything from rum-running to how Americans perceived Canadians as a race of Mounties and Eskimos. In anticipation of another summer of strife between Grace and Ernest, his father wrote him that month to say: "Do hope dear Ernest that you will think more of what others have done for you and try to be charitable and kind and gentle. Do not doubt that I am proud of your ability and your independence, but try to soften your temper and never threaten your Father and Mother. . . . I want you to represent all that is good and noble and brave and courteous in manhood, and fear God and respect Woman."[3]

Clarence Hemingway made a brief visit to the cottage in early July, handing Ernest a list of chores and sources for possible summer jobs. But after his father's two-week visit, Ernest, who would turn twenty-one that month, resumed his usual summer activities: writing, fishing, drinking, pursuing women (Katy Smith, in particular, although he also continued writing to Bonnie Bonnell in Toronto). As usual, he avoided all manual labor and domestic chores. A flurry of letters between Grace and Clarence reveals an attempt to analyze the problem. "I think Ernest is trying to irritate us in some way," Dr. Hemingway concluded.[4] Part of the source of irritation was that his son had invited his friend Ted Brumback to visit the cottage. Ernest's younger sisters Ursula and Sunny persuaded him and Ted to sneak out at midnight one night and accompany them on an all-night picnic, along with the two young Loomis girls from a neighboring cottage. Although the party was innocent enough, the idea of young girls being out all night with two grown men sparked a local scandal — especially when Mrs. Loomis knocked on Grace's door at three o'clock in the morning demanding to know where her daughters had gone. When Ernest and the others returned at dawn, Grace and Mrs. Loomis were waiting at the dock. "The air was blue with condemnations," Sunny Hemingway recalled.[5] Mrs. Loomis swore she would pack up her family and leave the lake unless Grace "could do something about those grown men loafing around."[6] Grace also had strong words for Ernest, but Ernest had a few of his own: "Of course Ernest called me every name in the book and said every vile thing about me," Grace wrote to her husband. "But I kept my tongue and did not get hysterical."[7]

The next day his mother called him into the living room and banished him from the cottage for good. She handed him a long letter that compared a parent–child relationship to a bank account and made it clear that his credit was bad:

> Unless you, my son Ernest, come to yourself, cease your lazy loafing and pleasure seeking — borrowing with no thought of returning — stop trying to graft a living off anybody and everybody — spending all your earnings lavishly and wastefully on luxuries for yourself — stop trading on your handsome face, to fool little gullible girls, and neglecting your duties to God and Your Savior, Jesus Christ — unless in other words, you come into your manhood, there is nothing before you but bankruptcy: You have over drawn.[8]

Ernest moved into a Chicago apartment with his ambulance service friend Bill Horne and continued to pursue his dreams of becoming a writer. He kept circulating his short fiction, but, as hard as he tried, the only money he could earn was that from the steady stream of freelance pieces he sent to the *Toronto Star*. Hemingway discussed his literary ambitions in frequent letters to Greg Clark, who urged him to forget fiction and concentrate his efforts where his true talent — and his brilliant future — lay: as a writer of colorful puff pieces for a weekend newspaper supplement.

Greg Clark wasn't the only *Star* editor who saw big things for Hemingway as a newspaper feature writer. The *Daily Star*'s managing editor, John Bone, was also developing an interest in young Hemingway, for reasons that proved to be self-serving. Bone had made a deal with the *Star*'s publisher Joseph Atkinson, that let him pad his income in a way that infuriated the more junior writers. Bone secured a contract to make money on the side by writing freelance articles for several prominent British and American newspapers. The novel twist is that Bone did not write the stories himself. He had his secretary retype feature articles that other reporters had written for the *Star* or the *Star Weekly* and send them out to the foreign publications under the byline "John R. Bone." This now-unbelievable form of sanctioned plagiarism was perfectly legal under Canadian copyright laws of the 1920s, which were heavily stacked in favor of the publisher.

Greg Clark, appalled at the notion of a managing editor collecting money for the work of others, was designated by other staff writers to go to his father, Joseph Clark, the *Star*'s city editor, and try to put a stop to Bone's side deal. But the senior Clark explained that nothing could be done. "Atkinson is not paying Bone what he might command at some other paper," Joseph Clark told his son. "And tell the other boys they will be best advised not to make a fuss about it. It will look like a union — and they will just get themselves fired."[9]

There were two hitches in Bone's system. First, he could not crib material from prominent *Star* writers who were themselves well known to other newspapers editors and wire services. His side deal could work well only if Bone could steal work from a writer who was both highly talented and completely unknown. A writer like this new kid who signed his name Ernest M. Hemingway.

"Bone was bringing in all these promising young university men" to basically serve as ghostwriters for his U.S. and British freelancing, Greg Clark recalled. "But he was on the hunt all the time for exactly what Hemingway was — a bright, young unknown [because] as soon as you became known, then it became a little embarrassing to lift your copy and put a new lead on it. . . . If somebody became too distinguished, Bone then had to drop him and start looking for some younger fellows to bring up, in this technique that he followed."[10]

The other hitch in scalping Hemingway's copy was that the big U.S. and British papers weren't overly interested in stories out of Toronto. To make his deal truly lucrative, Bone would need to encourage his young unknown to relocate to a more exotic and newsworthy locale. A place like Paris. This explains, to a large degree, why Hemingway rose so quickly through the *Star* ranks, from a half-a-penny-per-word freelancer in 1920 to being hired by John Bone as the newspaper's first roving European correspondent in 1921. Many wondered why a more experienced and better-known reporter did not get the European posting. But the anonymity of the successful candidate makes perfect sense considering what John Bone was planning to do with the dispatches penned by his European reporter. During his European posting, Hemingway would do stories on everything from an interview with Mussolini to a report on the evacuation of Constantinople. "[These European stories] were all assigned by Bone," Clark said, "who then, if possible, would clip it and put a new lead on it and resell it as his own. If it hadn't been for Bone and his rip-and-resell policy, Greg Clark insisted, "there wasn't another newspaper in North America on which Hemingway could have had the chance to try his wings that he found on the *Star* — on account of John Bone's future as a foreign correspondent."[11]

So it was that, in February of 1921, Bone wrote to Hemingway in Chicago to offer him the post of European correspondent. Greg Clark wrote to Hemingway separately to advise him that Bone wanted him "hard." Clark told Hemingway, "The chief wants men to jazz up the paper. He hasn't any. He thinks of you."[12]

Bone hadn't counted on one other stumbling block, however — that Hemingway would ask for more money than Bone was willing to pay. Clark had advised his young friend to demand $90 a week, a salary that would have made him the highest-paid reporter on the paper. This was more than double the $40 a week that Hemingway was by this time earning in Chicago while turning out filler for the *Cooperative Commonwealth* magazine, which was nothing more than the house organ of a rather shady financial operation, the Cooperative Society of America. Although he was already growing to suspect the motives of his employer and despise his hack work for the *Cooperative Commonwealth*, Hemingway, in usual fashion, exaggerated both his salary and his love for his Chicago job in the response to Bone's job offer. "At present, I am making $75 a week at agreeable, though rather dull work," he wrote to Bone in March of 1921. "I would be glad to come with you at $85 a week and could report April 1."[13]

Bone wanted a talented and unknown ghostwriter, but not at the salary Hemingway was seeking. (Bone well knew, after all, that only a year earlier this Hemingway had been more than happy to churn out lengthy *Star Weekly* features at five dollars apiece.) Bone's response to Hemingway's rather outrageous offer was highly effective and shattering: he made no response at all.

Hemingway waited six months before he decided to patch things up with Bone and land the proffered European posting. It was now the fall of 1921 and things were not going well. Not only had Hemingway lost his steady Chicago paycheque after the *Cooperative Commonwealth* folded in scandal but he was now newly married to another "older woman," twenty-nine-year-old Hadley Richardson of St. Louis.

Ernest and Hadley first met at a Chicago party in October of 1921, at the apartment of Y.K. Smith,

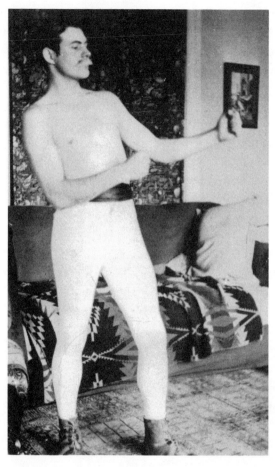

Hemingway strikes a boxing stance in the Chicago apartment of friend Y.K. Smith, in 1921.
(John F. Kennedy Library)

an advertising man who was Bill Smith's older brother. Ernest came in with Bill and Katy Smith, and Hadley found herself talking to a "hulky, bulky something masculine."[14] Ernest saw an attractive redhead who could play the piano brilliantly but seemed a little shy. As they talked, Ernest learned that Hadley's father had committed suicide in 1903 and her mother had died just that summer. Although Hadley was eight years older than Ernest — or perhaps *because* she was — Ernest felt a deep attraction. Hadley was on a 3-week visit to Chicago and she spent much of that time with Hemingway. When she returned home, they agreed to write each other, and the letters became increasingly romantic. Hemingway told her of his affections, and also told the story of his relationship with Agnes in Milan, who had loved him but then had "gone away." He told her he loved her and hoped to go on loving her "a little while at least."[15] But there were other women to think about. Bonnie Bonnell was still writing from Toronto, with letters that included Morse code messages that worked out to: "I Love You." And there was Katy Smith. And his friends told him he was much too young . . .

Hadley tried to counteract the gloomy tone of Ernest's notes by writing, "I do love you very much and can't think of anything unsympathetic about

Hadley Richardson was twenty-nine years old and felt herself destined to become a "spinster aunt" when she met the twenty-one-year-old Hemingway at a Chicago party in October 1920. The attraction was instant, and the couple was married the following summer. (John F. Kennedy Library)

you." She added that he was "always invited" to come and visit her in St. Louis.

On March 11 of 1921, Hemingway traveled to St. Louis to visit Hadley. She was unsure of the romance, but one of her friends, Ruth Bradfield, saw Ernest as "a beautiful youth. He was slender and moved well. His face had the symmetry of fine bone structure and he had a small elastic mouth that stretched from ear to ear when he laughed. . . . His focused attention to the person he was talking with was immensely flattering. . . . He generated excitement because he was so intense about everything, about writing and boxing, about good food and drink. Everything he did took on new importance when he was with us."[16] Hadley was similarly impressed with the way Ernest talked of writing, of sports, of war, with the way he blew his cigarette smoke. To back up his stories of war and writing, he showed her the two tokens he had brought along from Chicago: his Italian military cloak and his scrapbook full of *Toronto Star* articles, which Hadley read aloud to her friends.

The couple quickly became engaged. The impulsive nature of the decision soon gave Hemingway a case of cold feet and he became seriously depressed. By the summer, he was writing Hadley that he might kill himself, or, in his slang, "commit

Ernest and Hadley pose for wedding pictures in Horton Bay, Michigan, on September 3, 1921. Other members of the wedding party, from left to right, are Hemingway's sisters Carol and Ursula, his mother Grace, brother Leicester, and father Dr. Clarence Hemingway.

(John F. Kennedy Library)

mortage." Hadley wrote back on July 7 to say, "Old dear — what's this. *Not* truly so low as to crave mortage are you? The meanest thing I can say to you on that point is remember it would kill me to all intents and purposes. . . . Don't ever get confused when such a moment comes — don't ever forget that responsibility to me. You gotta live first for you and then for my happiness."[17] They were married on September 3, 1921.

Hemingway dreamed of taking his new love to Europe, to show her the Italy he now remembered so idyllically. But the collapse of the *Cooperative Commonwealth* job had left the newlywed Ernest with no means of support. Hemingway still had not made a single sale as a writer of fiction or poetry. The only thing to do was to go back, hat in hand, to Bone and beg for the European posting. Hemingway's October letter to Bone shows none of the cockiness of his earlier demands: "You very kindly suggested a position last February, but at the time I was getting some valuable experience and a very satisfactory salary here . . . and in answering your letter named a salary figure which was more, I believe, than you wished to pay."[18]

This was more the tone that John Bone liked to hear. By Thanksgiving, he and Hemingway had made a deal: Hemingway would go to Europe for the *Star* and write features on a freelance basis,

Star *managing editor John Bone hired Hemingway*
as a roving European reporter in November 1921.
Hemingway would be based in Paris and paid $75 a
week plus expenses while on assignment and
freelance rates for other articles. Hemingway, a
complete unknown, was perfect for the job, since
Bone often resold Star *reporters' work to U.S. papers*
under his own byline. (Toronto Star photo)

Hemingway had this passport photo taken in December 1921, to allow him and Hadley to sail for Paris so he could take up his new post as the Toronto Star's European correspondent.
(John F. Kennedy Library)

with all expenses paid. Hemingway would also be paid $75 a week as a staff writer when assigned to cover specific events, such as the upcoming conferences at Genoa and Lausanne, at which world leaders would assemble in a bid to sift through the political, diplomatic and economic shambles left in the aftermath of the Great War.

Hemingway and Hadley sailed for Europe on the *Leopoldina*, arriving on December 20, 1921, exactly two years from the day that Hemingway had prophetically written to his friend Howell Jenkins that "this Toronto thing looks like the original Peruvian Doughnuts."

CHAPTER 7

Roving Reporter,
1922

THE WEATHER WAS COLD AND MISERABLE AND A RAGING FLU epidemic was killing hundreds when Hemingway arrived in Paris to take up his new duties. Ernest and Hadley found a small, rather dingy apartment at 74 rue de Cardinal Lemoine, in the bohemian Latin Quarter. They went shopping for a tweed suit and shoes that Hemingway could wear to press conferences and interviews. But, only days after they settled into Paris life, they fled by overnight train to the ski slopes of Switzerland to escape the cold and, Ernest's greater fear, the threat of deadly disease. (He'd spent days in bed with a sore throat and, as always when illness was concerned, feared the worst.)

In the idyllic Alpine setting of Les Avants, Hemingway miraculously recovered and began churn-

*After finding an apartment in Paris, Ernest and
Hadley took a working vacation in Switzerland in
January 1922.* (John F. Kennedy Library)

ing out stories about bobsledding and tourists and
hanging around in hotels and basically anything
else that he felt like writing about. He made his
debut as a foreign correspondent with three pieces
in the *Star* of February 4, 1922.

After returning to their Paris apartment, Hemingway continued to produce dispatch after dis-

patch. John Bone may have believed he would save money by paying his roving correspondent on the basis of published output rather than basic salary. But within three months, Hemingway would go on to blitz his Toronto readers with some forty-six printed articles on everything from politics and economics to what sort of hat was currently fashionable on the boulevards of Paris (a sparrow hat).

In Europe, Hemingway found a whole new world of material to work with and, as always, showed a fine talent for manufacturing a human-interest story out of just about anything, largely because he never let the facts bog down a good yarn. He quickly learned one trick for writing his European features that he would later employ to infuse a sense of realism into his fiction: he realized that a writer did not have to experience an event first-hand to write; he had only to write vividly enough to make it *seem* as though he was reporting personal experiences.

"It is not unnatural that the best writers are liars," Hemingway would later explain. "A major part of their trade is to lie or invent and they will lie when they are drunk, or to themselves, or to strangers. They often lie unconsciously and then remember their lies with deep remorse. If they knew that all other writers were liars too it would cheer them up."[1]

Hemingway started writing *Star* articles that presented expert, firsthand accounts of things he had not seen or experienced. He took things he read in books and stories he overheard in cafés and bars and wrote about them as actual occurrences. In many ways, Hemingway's European articles for the *Star* were closer to fiction than to journalism.

For example, on the boat trip to France, Ernest and Hadley glimpsed the Spanish town of Vigo during a half-hour stopover. Hemingway noticed the boats in the harbor and was told that they were fishing for tuna. It was only a brief glimpse. He did not do any fishing in Vigo. But you would not know this by a report headlined "At Vigo, in Spain, Is Where You Catch the Silver and Blue Tuna, the King of All Fish," which appeared in the *Star* on February 18, 1922. After reading this report, which foreshadows the first-person perspective and detail of such future fiction as *The Old Man and the Sea*, no reader could know that Hemingway had not actually been on board, taking an active part in the tuna fishing:

> A big tuna is silver and slate-blue and when he shoots up into the air from close beside the boat it is like a blinding flash of quicksilver. He may weigh 300 pounds and he jumps with the eagerness and ferocity of a rain-

bow trout. Sometimes five and six tuna will be in the air at once in Vigo Bay, shouldering out of the water like porpoises as they herd the sardines, then leaping in a towering jump that is as clean and beautiful as the first leap of a well-hooked rainbow.

The Spanish boatmen will take you out to fish for them for a dollar a day. There are plenty of tuna and they take the bait. It is a back-sickening, sinew-straining, man-sized job even with a rod that looks like a hoe handle. But if you land a big tuna after a six-hour fight, fight him man against fish until your muscles are nauseated with the unceasing strain, and finally bring him up alongside the boat, green-blue and silver in the lazy ocean, you will be purified and will be able to enter unabashed into the presence of the very elder gods and they will make you welcome.

Dishonest? Perhaps. A good journalist supposedly has to learn to tell the truth. But being a good journalist was not Hemingway's ultimate goal. He was here to learn to write fiction and he was already beginning to understand that all good fiction writers had to be first-rate liars.

Although Hemingway had no French and had been in Paris only a few weeks, he was soon re-

porting on the expatriate bohemian scene in the
Latin Quarter with the jaded eye of the insider
who had seen it all once too often. Because of
the weak franc, American expatriates had flooded
into Paris, where they could use the favorable exchange rate to live and loaf very cheaply. By 1922
there were an estimated 35,000 Americans crowding the cafés of the Left Bank. And nearly every
one claimed to be a writer, artist or poet. Perhaps
the sight of these would-be writers reminded Hemingway all too well of his own unfulfilled literary
ambitions. In any case, his earliest *Star* dispatches
make it clear that he immediately distanced himself from the amateurs in the crowd. If there was
one thing that Hemingway could not stand to be
considered, it was an amateur. From the outset
he made it clear that he numbered himself among
the "real" artists of Paris. And it was from this
vantage point that he described the Latin Quarter
café life to his Toronto readers in an article that
ran in the *Star Weekly* on March 22, 1922, under
the headline "American Bohemians in Paris":

> The scum of Greenwich Village, New York, has
> been skimmed off and deposited in large la-
> dles on that section of Paris adjacent to the
> Café Rotonde. . . . They have striven so hard
> for a careless individuality of clothing that they

have achieved a sort of uniform of eccentricity. A first look at the smoky, high-ceilinged, table-crammed interior of the Rotonde gives you the same feeling that hits you as you step into the bird-house of a zoo. There seems to be a tremendous, raucous, many-pitched squawking going on, broken up by many waiters who fly through the smoke like so many black and white magpies. . . . You can find anything you are looking for at the Rotonde except serious artists . . . for the artists of Paris who are turning out credible work resent and loathe the Rotonde crowd. . . . They are nearly all loafers . . . talking about what they are going to do and condemning the work of all artists who have gained any degree of recognition. By talking about art, they obtain the same satisfaction that the real artist does in his work. That is very pleasant, of course, but they insist on posing as artists.

Since the days when Charles Baudelaire led a purple lobster on a leash through the same old Latin Quarter, there has not been much good poetry written in cafés.

Hemingway was implying that, as a professional, he would never dream of adopting a bohemian look or writing in a café. Within a year, however

— once he had sold his very first poem to a magazine — strollers on the Left Bank could easily find Ernest Hemingway front and center in the cafés of the Latin Quarter, looking distinctly bohemian as he scribbled away in his blue-covered notebooks.

Hemingway's shift in attitude about bohemian life is reflected in an unpublished fragment apparently intended for inclusion in his Paris memoir, *A Moveable Feast*, in which he looks back rather wistfully from the vantage point of late middle age on his time in Paris, remembering a twenty-two-year-old foreign correspondent and would-be writer who was fast becoming far too literary for the conventional foreign correspondents he rubbed elbows with by day:

> As long as I did newspaper work and had to go to different parts of Europe on assignments it was necessary to have one presentable suit, go to barbers, and have one pair of respectable shoes. These were a liability when I was trying to write because they made it possible to leave your own side of the river and go over to the right bank and see your friends there, go to the races, and do all the things that were fun and you could not afford or that got you into trouble. I found out very quickly that the best

way to avoid going over to the right bank and
get involved in all the pleasant things that I
could not afford and that left me with, at the
least, gastric remorse, was not to get a haircut.
You could not go over to the right bank with
your hair cut like one of those wonderful Japanese noblemen painters who were friends of
Ezra [Pound]'s.

Sometimes I would run into foreign correspondents that I knew when they were slum-
ming in what they thought of as the Quarter
and one would take me aside and talk to me
seriously, for my own good.

"You mustn't let yourself go, Hem. It's none
of my business, of course. But you can't go
native this way. For God's sake straighten out
and get a proper haircut at least."

Then if I was ordered to some conference
in Germany or the Near East I would have to
get a haircut and wear my one passable suit
and my good English shoes and sooner or later
I would meet the man who had straightened
me out and he'd say:

"You're looking fit old boy. Dropped that
bohemian nonsense I see. What are you up
to tonight? There's a very good place, absolutely special, up beyond Maxim's."

People who interfered in your life always did

it for your own good and I figured it out finally that what they wanted was for you to conform completely and never differ from some accepted surface standard and then dissipate the way traveling salesmen would at a convention.[2]

Hemingway had to learn to write quickly and sparely to keep up with the demands from his editors when on assignment for the *Star*. (He complained that he was expected to single-handedly cover conferences that other newspapers and news services sent whole teams to report on, but part of the problem was that he was already beginning to moonlight for other wire services under the by-line John Hadley — an ironic twist to John Bone's best-laid plans.)

In April 1922, Hemingway was sent to Italy to cover the Genoa Economic Conference, giving the young correspondent a front-row seat at one of the most important political summits of the decade. In Genoa, all the big players of Europe converged to seek a path to recovery from the staggering postwar recession. But there were much bigger agendas at play here, including the arrival of an officially unrecognized delegation of Russian Bolsheviks.

At Genoa, Hemingway ran the risk of being overwhelmed by the complexity of an ever-shifting po-

*While covering the Genoa Economic Conference for
the* Star *in 1922, Hemingway met journalist Lincoln
Steffens — and discovered that newspaper "cablese"
could be the basis for a new form of lean, stripped
down fiction.* (John F. Kennedy Library)

litical power struggle. Knowing the value of expertise, he quickly wangled his way into a group
of more seasoned newsmen and began picking
their brains to lend authority to the blizzard of
news reports he began sending to Toronto. Here

he met the legendary Lincoln Steffens, the famous, fifty-six-year-old muck-racking journalist who invited Hemingway and other young admirers to dine and drink with him in the proletariat quarter of Genoa in a café with the words "Viva Lenin" scrawled on the walls.

To the surprise of the veteran journalists, Ernest used these drinking sessions to speak in glowing and exuberant terms of a whole new way of writing that he was discovering while filing his *Star* dispatches — "cablese." To the others, the stripped-down, skeletal style of cablese was merely a way to cut down on wire costs by eliminating unnecessary adverbs and adjectives. But to Hemingway, who was new to the method, cablese was a revelation. More than a neat trick for journalists, it struck him as one of those few true eureka experiences in an all too short life.

One April night Hemingway showed Lincoln Steffens a *Toronto Star* dispatch he had written in cablese. Steffens scanned it and said, yes, he "saw the picture" of the newspaper story clearly. But Hemingway, as fellow journalist George Seldes recalled, "was not interested in what Steffens 'saw.' Hemingway was amazed and delighted with discovering a new way of writing English — he was fascinated by cablese." Hemingway pushed the story back to Steffens, urging him to forget the content of the dispatch. "Read the cablese, only the cablese," he told Steffens. "Isn't it a great language?"

As they talked and drank — usually having no trouble finishing a two-gallon jug of wine among four journalists — Steffens expounded on his famed view that he had "seen the future and it was Bolshevik Russia." "Was Hem impressed by Stef's radicalism?" Seldes later wondered. "I don't know. I don't think so. . . . The big discovery was cablese."[3]

Hemingway may have relied on his veteran friends to teach him the ins and outs of international politics and posturing, but he needed nobody's help in digging up human-interest subjects. (One of his less-than-hard-hitting reports is headlined "Two Russian Girls the Best-Looking at Genoa Parley.") *Dateline, Toronto* contains twenty-six stories with a Genoa dateline, but there are two more, published here for the first time. The two new stories are headlined "Genoa Scrubs Up for Peace Parley" and "Interpreters Make or Mar Speeches at Genoa Parley." (See Appendices 7 and 8.) Both appeared under the now familiar byline "Ernest M. Hemingway, Special Correspondence of The Star" on April 15, 1922.

In the first, Hemingway colorfully describes the working conditions for a journalist in the old city, making sure that his description adhered to Toronto's sober Protestant work ethic by carefully avoiding any mention of the nightly jugs of red wine that he shared with his fellow foreign reporters:

> The old Roman quarter of Genoa has the narrowest streets in the world. Most of them are not wide enough for good sized sidewalks, and the buildings rise five stories high, bulging out and nearly meeting at the top. . . .
>
> The hills of Genoa are so steep and the road so tortuous and congested that any sort of travel on wheels is very unpleasant. The cobbles jolt, the busses lurch, the people in the streets point at the bus with its official coat of arms, and wonder which of the forty some nations at the conference are riding in it.
>
> Press headquarters is in a palace in the heart of the city, and is full of a throng of men all speaking different languages, and all pounding ridiculously small typewriters with a look of concentration on their faces, or else writing in illegible longhand at the twenty tables scattered over the room. An elaborate bar has been fitted up with rows of bottles of Scotch, Irish and American rye whiskey, but it is deserted except for an occasional journalist who rushes

in and demands a glass of milk and a sandwich. Genoa is not a drinking conference. There is too much work to do, the delegations are scattered fifteen and twenty miles apart along the coast, and the newspapermen work like street laborers twelve and fifteen hours a day.

In the other uncollected story, "Interpreters Make or Mar Speeches at Genoa Parley," Hemingway complains about the inability of conference interpreters to accurately convey the original passion of the words of the delegates.

Chancellor Wirth, of Germany, lost almost the entire effectiveness of his very able speech at the opening of the conference because the interpreter garbled the words in such a manner they were absolutely impossible to understand in either French or English. Only those who understood German in the hall knew what Wirth had said. . . .

Wirth's interpreter was a wild-haired, wild-eyed young man, who, someone whispered in the press gallery while he was talking, was born in Chicago and spoke 22 languages. I believe he speaks them all equally badly.

Tchitcherin of the Russian delegation, Hemingway reports, was wise enough to speak in French "when he had some rapid-fire controversy on. . . . In this way Tchitcherin was sure that he would secure correct reporting of his speech." Hemingway is implying that he is one of the press gallery veterans who was fluent in enough languages to know a bad translation when he heard one. In fact, he spoke no German, and his French and Italian were limited to the words necessary to order drinks in cafés. It was Hadley, with her formal French schooling, who was the real communicator when French was required during the course of their Paris living. But these were things that a would-be insider could never admit.

CHAPTER 8

Under the Influence

IT IS A TESTAMENT TO HEMINGWAY'S CHARMS AND CONNEC-
tions that he soon became an accepted member
of the Paris literary scene after arriving in 1922,
without any published material to account for his
reputation as a writer to watch. Armed with a letter
of introduction from Chicago novelist Sherwood
Anderson, Hemingway befriended such Paris literary powers as Ezra Pound, Gertrude Stein, Sylvia
Beach and James Joyce. He also profited from
being lucky enough to have arrived in Paris at the
moment when the modernist movement in literature was being born, with both James Joyce's
Ulysses and T.S. Eliot's *The Waste Land* being published just blocks from Hemingway's apartment.
He played the role of student and disciple, learning
whatever he could from each of his new

In March 1922, Hemingway met Alice B. Toklas, left, and Gertrude Stein, pictured in Stein's Paris home. From Stein, Hemingway learned to use repetition of words to create an echo effect in his prose. After reading his fiction, Stein advised him to "stick to poetry."
(Photo by Man Ray)

*Paris bookstore owner Sylvia Beach, left, privately
published* Ulysses *by James Joyce, right. Her
Shakespeare & Company shop became a favorite
Paris haunt for Hemingway. Beach introduced
Hemingway to Joyce, who offered valuable advice
during numerous drinking sessions.*
(Photo by Man Ray)

friends. Ezra Pound helped Hemingway with his
poetry and prose, explaining his own imagist the-
ories on how to capture the poetic essence of a
scene. It was through Pound's recommendation
that Hemingway's first works appeared in such literary reviews as *Exile* and *The Little Review*. In re-

turn, Hemingway taught Pound to box. James Joyce read Hemingway's unpublished stories and instructed him not to state his meaning but to suggest it by holding back many of the critical details of a story. This allowed Hemingway to develop what he called his "iceberg theory" of fiction. "I always try to write on the principle of the iceberg," he later wrote. "There is seven eighths of it under water for every part that shows. Anything you know you can eliminate and it only strengthens the iceberg."[1] Hemingway became one of Joyce's drinking partners and would often help Joyce home when he'd had several too many. Nora Joyce would open the door on many occasions and exclaim, "Well, here comes James Joyce the writer, drunk again with Ernest Hemingway."[2]

Gertrude Stein taught him about the rhythm of prose and how to use repeated words to create a haunting echo effect. But the best advice she ever gave him, Hemingway claimed, was to quit journalism. In return for her help, Hemingway helped her publish her epic *The Making of Americans*, sneaking it as a serial into the *Transatlantic Review* when editor Ford Madox Ford left Hemingway in charge of the magazine in the summer of 1924. All these factors helped shape Hemingway's style. He later rejected Stein's influence, saying that she told him "a lot of shit" mixed in with

Ernest and Hadley took a walking trip in the Black Forest of Germany in August 1922, an experience that Hemingway recorded in several Toronto Star *articles.* (John F. Kennedy Library)

a few useful things,[3] and that it was he who taught her how to write. This is characteristic of Hemingway, who later rejected many of his literary benefactors. Pound and Joyce were two notable exceptions.

In September of 1922, Hemingway traveled to St. Vincent du Jard, in the south of France, with veteran reporter Bill Bird, to interview Georges Clemenceau, the eighty-year-old "Tiger of France," a war hero who was due to make a speaking tour of North America. By now, fast at work on developing his fiction, Hemingway was clearly using his *Star* dispatches as an opportunity to experiment with short story techniques. His vivid report of his visit with Clemenceau carefully describes the countryside, the furnishings of the house and many other sharp details:

> The room was of plain boards. On one side was a wash stand with a basin and pitcher, on the other a writing desk. In back of the sofa where I sat was a comfortable bed. Over the bed was a bookcase. On the wall, the only ornaments were the mounted heads of antelope and buck Clemenceau had shot on his trip to India. Over the writing desk was a big crocodile's head with open jaws and silly-looking glass eyes. But the thing that caught and held your eye was a tiger skull that was nailed up over the window and facing the sea. It was bone white and polished and the two big teeth coming down represented the Cle-

menceau mustache. It looked exactly like the cartoons of the Old Tiger himself.

Hemingway does not even introduce the subject of his interview until several hundred words into his report, but his description of his first glimpse of Clemenceau smacks of the repetition of words and rhythm of the early Hemingway literary style.

I had gotten up to look at the titles of the books on the shelf above the writing desk and had only noted one, "The History Of Buddhism" when we heard voices coming from the back of the cottage. Round the corner of the cottage, walking in the deep sand, came Clemenceau's son and Clemenceau himself walking with the son's wife, his arm through hers. A bulky man, thickened by age, wearing a brown tweed suit, a funny, flat cap, his face as brown as an Ojibway, his white mustache drooping, his white eye-brows bushy, looking the tiger his pictures show him, his eyes twinkling as he talked to his plump daughter-in-law, he came plodding through the sand. They stopped in front of the door. "Au revoir papa!" The woman bent toward him to kiss him. Clemenceau put his arms around her and kissed her.

"Au revoir, my child. See you soon." They went on to their car and he came plodding into the room. His eyes smiled. They are the only things you can see while you are talking to him. They seem to get inside of your eyes somehow and fasten claws there. When he is talking all his brown, healthy, Chinese mandarin's face seems to have nothing to do with them. But his eyes smiled at us.[4]

Despite the excellent color, the *Star*'s John Bone rejected the Clemenceau story, citing a brief passage in the story in which Clemenceau makes an insulting and erroneous reference to Canadians being unwilling to fight during World War I. "I don't understand why Clemenceau should say that the Canadians objected to compulsory service and refused to help France," Bone wrote to Hemingway in his letter of rejection. "As his reference to Canada constitutes the most interesting part of the interview, I don't think we should use it at all."[5]

The story has never been collected or published until now. The complete version can be found in Appendix 10.

Over the next year, Hemingway continued in his fascination with breaking sentences down to their barest bones and sinews. And, in doing this, he created a series of vignettes published in December 1923 by American writer and publisher Robert McAlmon's small Paris press, Contact Editions, under the title *in our time*. As comparison of one of his Near East dispatches for the *Star* with a vignette that later appeared in *in our time* indicates, he often distilled his journalism into fiction. In October of 1922, the *Star* sent Hemingway to the Near East to cover the Greco-Turkish fighting. The Turks, under Kemal Pasha, were closing in for the kill on Constantinople. Hemingway filed a vivid "first person" account of the evacuation of a bedraggled and dispirited line of Christian refugees, (although he did not actually witness the event but merely read a newspaper account). His report appeared in the *Daily Star* of October 20, 1922, under the headline "A Silent Ghastly Procession Wends Way from Thrace":

> In a never-ending, staggering march, the Christian population of Eastern Thrace is jamming the roads toward Macedonia. The main column crossing the Maritza River at Adrianople is twenty miles long. Twenty miles of carts drawn by cows, bullocks and muddy-flanked water buffalo, with exhausted, staggering men, women and children, blankets over their heads, walking blindly along in the rain beside

all their worldly goods. . . . Now they can only keep their places in the ghastly procession while mud-splashed Greek cavalry herd them along like cow-punchers driving steers. . . . A husband spreads a blanket over a woman in labor in one of the carts to keep off the driving rain. She is the only person making a sound. Her little daughter looks at her in horror and begins to cry. And the procession keeps moving.

Hemingway would compress this *Star* article to create one of his short literary sketches. He not only distilled the 241-word article to a 132-word sketch but also cut out twenty of the original thirty adjectives, along with many of the phrases, such as "ghastly" or "in horror," that were meant to tell readers how to react emotionally. "When journalism was transformed to literature," wrote Scott Donaldson, "the signposts fell away along with much of the verbiage."[6] The finished version became the second chapter of his book *in our time.*

Minarets stuck up in the rain out of Adrianople across the mud flats. The carts were jammed for thirty miles along the Karagatch road. Water buffalo and cattle were hauling carts through the mud. No end and no beginning. Just carts loaded with everything they owned. The old men and women, soaked through, walked along keeping the cattle moving. The Maritza was running yellow almost up to the bridge. Carts were jammed solid on the bridge with camels bobbing along through them. Greek cavalry herded along the procession. Women and kids were in the carts crouched with mattresses, mirrors, sewing machines, bundles. There was a woman having a kid with a young girl holding a blanket over her and crying. Scared sick looking at it. It rained all through the evacuation.

Later Hemingway perfected this style of lean short sentences in *The Sun Also Rises* and other works, a style that his friend, author John Dos Passos, aptly described as being based "on cablese and the King James Bible."

Hemingway's coverage of the Greco-Turkish War produced fourteen articles for the *Star* but was also the source of many works of fiction. The coverage was "immensely important to his development as a writer," biographer Jeffrey Meyers wrote. "The war inspired three superb vignettes from his first mature work, *in our time* (1924), which were as good, stylistically, as anything he wrote; a reference in the deleted conclusion to 'Big Two-Hearted

River' (1925), 'On the Quai at Smyrna' (1930), two passages in *Death in the Afternoon* (1932), and two crucial flashbacks in his greatest story, 'The Snows of Kilimanjaro' (1936). The retreat from Caporetto in *A Farewell to Arms* (1929) and the plight of the Spanish Civil War refugee in 'The Old Man at the Bridge' (1938), also recall the Greek retreat through Eastern Thrace."[7]

He continued in his journalistic double-dealing, copying his *Toronto Star* wires to the International News Serivce. It was to Frank Mason of INS that Hemingway wired perhaps his most famous bit of cablese. When Mason contacted Hemingway about some mix-up in the books over expenses. Hemingway fired back a telegram that read, "SUGGEST YOU UPSTICK BOOKS ASSWARDS."[8]

But Hemingway's side deal with INS had not escaped the eye of the wily John Bone, who kept a close watch on stories appearing in American newspapers and began to notice numerous duplications of Hemingway's work under the byline John Hadley. When Bone wrote to Hemingway asking for an explanation, Hemingway wrote back to offer the rather feeble excuse that Mason of INS had been stealing his copy. Hemingway claimed that, stranded miles from a telegraph office while in Constantinople, he had given his story to an army officer who had in turn sent it to Mason in Paris, with instructions to relay it by wire to the *Star*. "Mason's office relayed it promptly but proceeded to steal and rewrite as much of it as they could get away with. I placed more confidence in Mason's honesty than it deserved. At any rate I have had it out with Mason. It was a personal matter and a question of ethics. . . . I was disgusted with the matter."[9]

Bone, of course, would have quickly seen through this excuse because he knew of seven other stories that had been "stolen" by INS in the same manner as this one.

Hemingway's double-dealing had escalated into triple-dealing by the time he covered the Lausanne peace conference in December of 1922. By that time, he was not only moonlighting for the INS wire service but also filing dispatches for the rival UPS news service — and collecting salaries and expense money from three sources at once. But it was no easy task to be "running a twenty-four-hour wire service for an afternoon and morning news service under two different names."[10] Reporters were barred from the talks and could find out what happened only by reading between the lines of the flurry of official press releases that each delegation issued each day. It was boring work, rewriting press handouts into spot news dispatches, and also time-consuming, so much so that Hemingway did not get around to filing reports for his main employer, the *Toronto Star*, until late January of 1923, long after the Lausanne conference had ended. His entire output for the *Star* consisted of two dispatches, both written in January, including a profile of Italian fascist leader Benito Mussolini (whom Hemingway pegged as "Europe's prize bluffer").

While covering the Lausanne conference for the *Star*, Hemingway invited Hadley to join him for a Swiss vacation. He added that he had shown Lincoln Steffens some of his short stories in progress, among them "My Old Man" and "Up in Michigan." To Hemingway's delight, the older writer both praised the stories and offered to send "My Old Man" to a prominent magazine editor. Delighted by her husband's apparent breakthrough after so many years of disappointment, Hadley planned a surprise for Ernest. She gathered up all his fictional works in progress — short stories, poems and even a partially completed war novel — and packed them in her suitcase to take to Switzerland so that Hemingway would have more material to show to his influential friends. But Hemingway got a surprise of a different nature when Hadley got off the train in Lausanne: after hours of weeping, she finally worked up the nerve to tell her husband that her suitcase — and all of his stories — had been stolen at the Paris train station. As Hemingway described it in his Paris memoir, *A Moveable Feast*:

> I had never seen anyone hurt by a thing other than death or unbearable suffering except Hadley when she told me about the things being gone. She had cried and cried and could not tell me. I told her that no matter what the dreadful thing was that had happened nothing could be that bad, and whatever it was, it was all right and not to worry. We would work it out. Then, finally, she told me. I was sure she could not have brought the carbons too and I hired someone to cover for me on my newspaper job. I was making good money then at journalism, and took the train for Paris. It was true all right and I remember what I did in the night after I let myself into the flat and found it was true.[11]

Not all was lost. Hemingway still had three short stories that were in the hands of various friends, including Steffens and Greg Clark. And much of his very early work was in boxes at his Oak Park home. And much of what was lost was material that perhaps deserved to be discarded. But Hadley's carelessness with his work was something that

Hemingway would never fully get over. It was a mistake from which their marriage would never recover.

There was good news mixed with the bad, however. It was during this time in 1922 as a roving *Star* reporter that Hemingway at last sold his first literary work, a single short poem to the *Double Dealer*, followed quickly by a six-poem series to *poetry magazine*. After three years of hard work and frustrating rejection, Hemingway could finally call himself a published literary writer.

When not on assignment Hemingway lived the expatriate life to the hilt, writing his fiction and poems in cafés, betting on the horse and bike races, eating well, drinking even better. To his delight, Hadley could hold her own in the drinking department. They would regularly drink a bottle of wine each at lunch, have aperitifs and cocktails in the afternoon and polish off two more bottles of wine each at dinner. Between the two of them, they could (and regularly did) drink just about all of the Paris expatriate set under the fashionable café tables of the Latin Quarter.

In February 1923, the Hemingways visited Ezra Pound, who was wintering in Rapallo, Italy. It was a nice vacation from the news business, but it was in Rapallo that Hadley broke her own bit of news: she was pregnant. It came as a shock to Ernest, since the baby was not planned. "I'm too young to be a father," he complained to Gertrude Stein.[12] Paris had been a lot of fun, and the writing was going well and now this: a child could clearly put a damper on all the fun. Especially since Hadley did not trust the Paris hospitals. She wanted to have the baby in Toronto.

John Bone had been disappointed with Hemingway's production at the Lausanne conference. And perhaps Hemingway felt some guilt of his own, because he tackled his next assignment — a six-week tour of Germany's occupied Ruhr district — with an energy that produced some of his best work as a foreign correspondent. The *Star* published six of the ten Ruhr stories on the front page and gave prominent play to the other four. John Bone was not the only one impressed with the series. Hemingway's father also wrote to offer congratulations. His son replied, "I'm glad you liked the Franco-German articles. They handle the show pretty well, at least make it an actual thing to people instead of simply a name on a map."[13]

Encouraged by his correspondent's new-found energy, Bone wrote to suggest that Hemingway leave Paris and set up headquarters in Moscow for

Hemingway saw his first bullfights on a trip to Spain over the summer of 1923. When the first bull entered the ring, Hemingway was hooked for life. "Then he charged," he wrote in one of two Toronto Star *features, "and as he charged, I suddenly saw what bullfighting is all about."*
(John F. Kennedy Library)

an extended look at life in post-czarist Russia. But Hadley — who had fought bitterly with Ernest over his trip to cover the war in Turkey — would not hear of a move to Russia now that she was expecting. Hemingway wired Bone: "RUSSIA UNFEASIBLE FOR ME AT PRESENT UNLESS EMERGENCY."[14]

Hemingway had his own reasons for balking at the Russia assignment. In Lausanne and the Ruhr, he had earned enough money — thanks to hard work and double-dealing — to afford to suspend his newspaper work for the entire summer of 1923. This would give him a chance to get back to his long-neglected fiction writing, as well as allow him to take his first look at Spain, to attend a fiesta and go to a bullfight and do some other things he had never done before.

Hemingway first saw a bullfight in Spain with his friend the artist Mike Strater. Leaving Hadley behind, they took the train from Paris to Madrid only to find the bullring completely sold out. But after much negotiating in broken French, they managed to buy ringside seats from scalpers for twenty-five pesetas apiece. The seats were right above the royal box and the chute where the bulls charged out into the bright afternoon sunshine. There was much pageantry and ceremony. And then the bullfight began. It was a spectacle that

Hemingway would never forget. He recorded this first impression in a *Star Weekly* article, "Bull Fighting Is Not a Sport — It Is a Tragedy," published October 20, 1923.

> Ducking his head as he came out of the dark pen, a bull came into the arena. He came out all in a rush, big, black and white, weighing over a ton, and moving with a soft gallop. Just as he came out the sun seemed to dazzle him for an instant. He stood as though he were frozen, his great crest of muscle up, firmly planted, his eyes looking around, his horns pointed forward, black and white and sharp as porcupine quills. Then he charged. And as he charged, I suddenly saw what bullfighting is all about. For the bull was absolutely unbelievable. He seemed like some great prehistoric animal, absolutely deadly and absolutely vicious. . . . "Ole" — pronounced Oh-Lay! — roared the crowd.

In July, Hemingway made a second trip to Spain, this time with Hadley, to attend the bullfights in Pamplona. Here Hemingway witnessed for the first time the running of the bulls through the Pamplona streets. In the *Star Weekly* article "World Se-

Hemingway and Paris small press publisher Robert
McAlmon attended the bullfights in Pamplona,
Spain, in the summer of 1923. McAlmon, moved by
the story of Hemingway's lost suitcase of stories,
published the surviving material in Hemingway's
first book, Three Stories & Ten Poems.
(John F. Kennedy Library)

ries of Bull Fighting a Mad, Whirling Carnival,"
which appeared October 27, 1923, he vividly
evokes this dramatic scene:

Down the narrow fenced-in runway came a crowd of men and boys running, running as hard as they could go. The gate feeding into the bullring was opened and they all ran pell-mell under the entrance levels, into the ring. Then came another crowd, running even harder. Straight up the long pen from the town. . . . Then they came in sight. Eight bulls galloping along, full-tilt, heavyset, black, glistening, sinister, their horns bare, tossing their heads. . . . And running ahead of them sprinted, tore, ran and bolted the rear guard of the men and boys of Pamplona who had allowed themselves to be chased through the streets for a morning's pleasure.

These two long *Star Weekly* bullfighting articles were Hemingway's first printed words on a ritual that would become a life-long obsession. His second novel, *The Sun Also Rises*, is partially set in Pamplona.

With Hadley due to give birth in October, the *Star* offered Hemingway a job on the local staff of the *Star*'s daily edition. The Toronto doctors were noted for their record of delivering babies safely. And both John Bone and Greg Clark told Hemingway that he could truly make a name for himself as the resident star of the local staff. The decision to return to Toronto in late August of 1923 was made. But it could not have been easy for Hemingway, just as things were starting to happen in his literary career. Dismayed by his story of the lost suitcase, Robert McAlmon had brought out a privately printed edition of Hemingway's remaining work, which amounted to three stories and ten poems. The book, published just before Ernest and Hadley sailed for Canada, was entitled, aptly enough, *Three Stories & Ten Poems*.

CHAPTER 9

A Star Returns,
1923

ON AUGUST 26, 1923, ERNEST AND HADLEY SAILED FOR CANADA from Cherbourg aboard the Cunard liner *Andania*. Hadley, now almost eight months pregnant, spent most of the stormy, ten-day trip in their cabin, feeling sick. As the ship steamed up the St. Lawrence River for Montreal, Hemingway was already regretting the decision to leave Paris and, yearning for the French way of life, had to resist an urge to jump ship in Quebec City and live there until the money ran out. On disembarking in Montreal, he was handed a letter from John Bone, welcoming him "home" and adding, "We shall be glad to see you in Toronto as soon as possible."[1] Greg Clark had also written, enthusing about the wonderful and leisurely time that Hemingway was about to have as a highly paid feature writer. "The paper needs you bad," Clark wrote, "and you will be in a position to tear into things here and write your name in the skies."[2]

Despite the warm welcome, Hemingway had already sunk into a bad mood by the time the train arrived in Toronto. After several years of artistic freedom in Europe, the clean, sober Protestant city in which he was planning to spend the next two years reminded him all too much of the churchy lifestyle of mother Grace. Perhaps Wyndham Lewis, who was marooned in Toronto during World War II, said it best when he described the city as a "sanctimonious icebox" where the Presbyterians and Methodists created "a reign of terror for the toper and the whoremaster. . . . If New York is brutal and babylonian, in this place it is as if some one were sitting on your chest — having taken the care to gag you first — and were croaking out [hymns] . . . from dawn to dayshut."[3]

In early September Hemingway fired off the first of many letters to Ezra Pound becrying his fate. He acknowledged that Toronto was "the right place to have a baby because that is the specialité de ville" but bemoaned the fact that he had not had a drink in five days, a condition that made him feel like crying. He could not sleep. As a diversion he read one of the many copies of James Joyce's *Ulysses* that he had smuggled in his suitcase in defiance of a North American ban on the book. "It [my situation] couldn't be any worse. You can't imagine it," he told Pound. "I start work on Monday."[4]

When he reported for work on September 10, 1923, Hemingway was expecting to do some celebrity feature writing and other plum assignments. But any enthusiasm he might have felt for his job soon dissipated. After checking the assignment ledger that morning, he whirled and stomped out of the office, trailing a stream of obscenities. He was about to undergo what the other staff members clearly recognized as "the Hindmarsh treatment."

Morley Callaghan, who would later join Hemingway's circle of writers in Paris, was then a part-time cub reporter. He had not yet met Hemingway but had heard whispered praise from deskman Jimmy Cowan. Cowan had told Callaghan that this Hemingway was "a real writer" and that he was coming back to Toronto from Europe to become the star of the local staff. Under John Bone's instructions, the *Star*'s promotion department had also heralded Hemingway's return with a blurb that trumpeted his exploits as a foreign correspondent, spoke of his "mastery" of both French and Italian and described his service with "the Italian forces" and his wounds and decorations. All were exaggerations. Hemingway had learned an impressive amount of French and Italian while in Europe but he was not yet a master of either. And of course he had never served with the Italian army.

On that first morning, Callaghan had hurried to check the ledger as soon as it had come out of the office of assistant managing editor Harry C. Hindmarsh. "I ran my eye down the page and saw Hemingway's name in at least five places," he later recalled. "Fascinated, I looked to see what kind of assignment was being given to the big correspondent from Europe." What Callaghan saw shocked him: "Five inconsequential jobs such as I might be asked to do myself! . . . They were piddling. Just junk assignments."[5]

Three and a half years earlier, Hemingway had spent his days perched on the radiator of Greg Clark's second-floor office, enjoying the slow pace and relative privacy and autonomy afforded to members of the *Star Weekly* staff. Hemingway had always been allowed to do as he pleased when he wrote for *Star Weekly* editor J.H. Cranston and even when he wandered Europe as a special correspondent under managing editor Bone. They knew he was a star and, to a large degree, they trusted him to dig up his own assignments and his own colorful angles on stories. But, with his return to Toronto, Hemingway was now a staff re-

Although he had been allowed the freedom to write whatever he pleased as a Star Weekly freelancer and European correspondent, Hemingway found himself under the thumb of Star city editor Harry Hindmarsh (at right at the city desk) when he joined the Daily Star staff on September 10, 1923. (Toronto Star photo)

porter for the *Daily Star*, and that put him under the direct command of Hindmarsh. Now he was working in the third-floor city room, where the pace was anything but casual and friendly. It was a large, dingy open space with a row of desks and a round table at the center where the city editor and three deskmen sat. Six days a week, reporters had to be at their desks at seven in the morning and ready to work until long into the night. There was no detailed style sheet to explain how a story should be written. The only advice that a *Star* reporter needed was posted in a note on the bulletin board: "Put a punch in every paragraph."

The newsroom buzzed with electric energy, for the *Star* was in an all-out battle with its rival, the *Toronto Telegram*. It was scoop or be scooped, and the *Star* would spare no cost — personal or financial — to score a victory over the *Tely*. And if this was war, there was no doubt who was the general.

Harry Comfort Hindmarsh was a brusque, beefy man of six foot two with a short military haircut and a stiff military bearing. He did not expect his reporters and editors to like him — in fact, he knew that most were scared stiff of him — but he did expect them to obey him without question. Hindmarsh's favorite tactic in his bitter struggle with the *Telegram* was the all-out assault: flying

The Star blitzed any newsworthy event with flying squads of reporters and then rushed the news out onto the streets in its bid to win a bitter circulation war with the Toronto Telegram. (Toronto Star photo)

squads of reporters would swarm the scene of any breaking news, local or international. In getting the story, *Star* reporters were in competition not only with their rivals but with each other. It was every man for himself. The reporter who could come up with a scoop was rewarded with an on-the-spot raise. The starting salary was $20 a week, and new employees were told that if they did not receive at least one substantial raise within three months, they should take it as a tip to quit. Reporters who did not take the hint to leave of their own accord were often fired on the spot. It was a dog-eat-dog atmosphere in the newsroom, and new *Daily Star* reporters like Ernest Hemingway would have been seen as just one more threat, one more rival to beat. "There was no welcoming committee [for new reporters] back then," said Roy Greenaway, a city reporter when Hemingway joined the Toronto staff. Any new man "resembled a stray cur who had usurped a place in the pack."

Greenaway related that it was Hindmarsh's method to break in any new man by "putting him in harness" — testing his endurance by driving him day and night until he quit, cracked up, was fired or landed in a detox center. "At any given time as many as four or five *Star* reporters . . . were temporarily taking 'the cure' in institutions," Greenaway said. "The cold fact remained that if a man could not take it, he could leave."[6] And if there was one thing that Hindmarsh would not tolerate, it was a prima donna. As Cranston later told biographer Charles Fenton, "Hindmarsh hated prima donnas, and it was his regular practice to reduce men to size by giving them more or less common assignments after they had done an outstanding piece of work and were proud of themselves. . . . He was ambitious, cruel and jealous of the success of others. . . . Hindmarsh was a driver, who expected implicit obedience from his men. He ruled by fear. . . . [He] was a sadist [who] took delight in breaking or humbling men's spirits."[7]

According to *Dateline, Toronto*, Hemingway's first story for the *Star* was published on September 25, 1923, fifteen days after he joined the local staff. But previously overlooked evidence indicates that Hemingway was turning out work from his very first day back on the job. A long, rather dry political piece headlined "Offer Sir Donald Soviet Railroads" (see Appendix 13), which appeared without a byline on September 10, is most certainly written by Hemingway.

Star records also suggest that the moment Hemingway completed the "Sir Donald" piece, he was sent to the railway station to catch the overnight

Infamous gangster Norman "Red" Ryan escaped from Kingston Penitentiary on Hemingway's first day on the Daily Star *staff. Ernest was sent to Kingston to cover the jailbreak. Although his dispatches received front page attention, he was not given bylines. (*Toronto Star *Archives)*

Pullman for Kingston, some 120 miles east of Toronto, to cover a jailbreak from the maximum-security Kingston Penitentiary. Notorious gangster Norman "Red" Ryan, who had been sentenced to twenty-five years and lashes for bank robbery, had violently attacked a guard with a pitchfork, tied up a hated convict in a burning building and scaled the wall with three other prisoners.

Ryan and the other cons were still at large the next morning when Hemingway caught up with the armed guards, who had been searching all night for the dangerous escapees. The colorful account of the manhunt, which appeared in the *Star* the next day, is not bylined but its style certainly suggests that it is Hemingway's. The sentences are terse and direct, and a Stein-like echo effect is created by the intentional repetition of words. Rather than merely interviewing the four guards, the author reconstructs their story to create the impression that he had actually been there, on horseback with them and their scout, as they stalked their quarry through the darkness along a road surrounded by heavy bush:

> It was so dark that the scout could not see his horse's head. But he heard the fence wires on the south side of the road creak. He shouted to the guards who were further down the road

and then there was silence. The four men had their rifles ready.

Then in the dark there was a rush across the road. The guards fired into the dark at the sound and rushed forward. In the dark a man's voice said, "Are you hurt, Shorty?" The guards shot again where the voice came from and one of them fired point blank as a man dashed by him toward the north side of the road. The men had crossed from the south tract of the woods to the northern half of the seven hundred acres. About fifteen rifle shots were fired in the dark. There was no blood and there are no bodies.

This report was carried on the front page of the September 11 *Star* under the banner headline, "Escaped Kingston Convicts Still at Large." (See Appendix 14.) It filled an entire column of page one and took up most of the second page. After filing this dispatch, Hemingway apparently stayed in Kingston for two more days, for three follow-up stories appeared on the front page: the first headlined "Convicts Set Fire to Stable at 'Pen' and Made Escape," the second "Provincial Police Are Taking Up Chase" and the third "Guards Hoaxed by Call for Help." All three of these stories are missing from the official Hemingway record. They are live-

On returning to Toronto in September 1923, Ernest and Hadley took a room in the Selby Hotel on Sherbourne Street. (Toronto Star photo)

ly accounts and they received prime play in the paper, but none of them has a byline. All are merely signed "Special to The Star by a Staff Reporter." As we shall see, denying a reporter proper credit for hard work was only one of Harry Hindmarsh's favorite tricks.

While Hemingway was in Kingston in search of Red Ryan and his gang, Hadley stayed at the Selby Hotel, a gabled Victorian building that had once been elegant but, like the other mansions on Sherbourne Street, was starting to decay now that the downtown core had shifted several blocks west to Yonge Street. The Selby would be their home until they could find a suitable apartment. To keep busy, Hadley read books — a volume of the love letters of Abelard and Héloise. She paid frequent visits to the Connable mansion, where Harriet Connable served as a surrogate mother and Dorothy — whom Hadley had once thought of as a rival for Ernest's attention — became Hadley's close friend.

Hadley and Ernest had thought that the *Toronto Star* job would allow them some time together. Yet Hemingway had arrived at work to find he had not even been assigned his own desk, let alone an office such as Greg Clark or other top reporters had. He was clearly going to have to do much of his work out of the office, even out of town.

Hadley was often left alone with her books after
Hemingway returned to Toronto to join the Daily
Star *staff. Appalled by Ernest's workload and his*
frequent out-of-town assignments, she wrote a
friend, "He is almost crazy . . . Staying is hell."
(John F. Kennedy Library)

Hindmarsh continued to hand out the most menial of assignments to Hemingway, the sort of
things that only apprentice reporters were usually
asked to do. The assistant managing editor would

Undergoing the "Hindmarsh Treatment,"
Hemingway was often handed vague assignments.
He would be told to head up Bay Street to the tower
of Toronto's city hall to "see what was going on."
(City of Toronto Archives)

send him out to pick up a photo of an accident victim from grieving family members or vaguely instruct him to "go over to city hall and see what was going on."[8] Hemingway went to work early in the morning and often did not come home until well past midnight, only to be jolted awake by a 3 a.m. phone call from the city desk, dispatching him to the scene of a fire.

By the middle of his first week on the job, Hemingway had already begun to show signs of exhaustion. But if he was hoping to rest during his weekend off, he soon realized this was wishful thinking. On Thursday, Hindmarsh decided to see how Hemingway would pan out as an investigative reporter. One of the hot stories of the day — at least as far as Hindmarsh was concerned — was a scheme by a shady company to swindle the public into investing in a dubious coal mine in Sudbury, Ontario. The company, British Colonial Coal Mines Ltd., had begun selling mining shares from an office in Toronto. Hindmarsh was convinced that one of the principals of the company, Alfred F.A. Coyne, was a crook; this opinion was bolstered by the fact that Coyne had already been charged with stock fraud in western Canada. Hemingway had had experience in working with shady dealers like Coyne during his days as a flack for the corrupt Cooperative Society of America in Chicago.

Perhaps because he felt duped by the Cooperative owners — who had him writing press releases assuring that all was well when in fact the investors were about to lose millions in securities — he went after the British Colonial Coal story with some zeal. The young journalist pored over the thick dossier of information that the *Star* had compiled on the suspect company and began to work through the weekend. Because it is such a lengthy feature, the British Coal story is not published in its entirety here. But this previously overlooked piece should nonetheless be added to the complete list of works written by Hemingway for the *Star*.

From the outset, Hemingway detected a suspicious odor emanating from the British Colonial Coal headquarters. He begins his story by pointing out that the company appears in the telephone directory as being located in the Temple Building, but strangely is not listed in the building's office directory. After some sleuthing he was apparently able to find the coal company president, Stewart Hood, working out of the eleventh-floor offices of National Finance, the company that was issuing the suspect mining stocks. Hood and National Finance president J.W. Henderson both agreed to grant Hemingway an interview. In his interview, Hood claims that the shady Alfred Coyne is no longer connected to the company and begins to give the young reporter the hard sell, but Hemingway's account — laced with a heavy dose of irony and sarcasm — makes it clear that the coal swindlers threw no dust in his eyes:

> Another man [Hood] in a brown suit, a hawk face, his hair parted at the side and a little inclined to hang dankly forward at the parting, commenced talking. He had a charming voice. He started right out speaking very slowly and convincingly and smiling quizzically.
>
> "There's something here I want to show you," he said. "Here are two pieces of coal. Look them over."
>
> He handed them to me. They looked identical. They might have come from the same coal pile.
>
> "Look them over," the soft soothing voice urged. "Examine them carefully."
>
> I looked them over and examined them carefully. They looked like coal. The voice went on. The smile continued. There was an effect that it had all been said before. It was all too smooth, frank, reasonable and so straightforward.
>
> "One of these pieces of coal," the voice continued, "is from Pennsylvania. The other," he paused, "is from Sudbury." He smiled at me.

Then in a smooth voice, accenting the word *which*, "Which is which?"

Naturally I didn't know. But it was an even money shot so I picked. "This one came from Sudbury," I said.

"That piece of coal," the voice purred on, "came from Pennsylvania."

Somehow I felt it had.[9]

Hemingway finished the story late on Sunday — his one day off — and left it for Hindmarsh along with a memo marked 12:30 a.m. in which he said he had written his piece "in detail with the atmosphere and the verbatim correspondence in case we get proof that they are crooks and you decide to do an exposure." Perhaps to prove that he was not the cub reporter that Hindmarsh seemed to take him for, Hemingway explained that the entire interview was conducted and recorded without notes and that he relied on his journalistic expertise and photographic memory for detail. "In a thing like this British Colonial it is impossible to take notes when you get them started contradicting etc., as to take out a pencil would shut them up tight."[10]

Hindmarsh rejected the story, fearing a libel suit.

The next morning Ernest found a memo from Hindmarsh, addressed to "Mr. Hemmingway." The memo concluded that the only way to get to the bottom of the coal scam was to send Hemingway to the Sudbury mining site on a junket with Coyne, who held stock not only in British Colonial but also in another new coal mine in the Sudbury basin.

Once again, Hemingway packed his bags for a long train ride. To alleviate the boredom he took along all the Joseph Conrad stories he could find. The barren landscape rolled by; the train stopped in small towns long enough for Hemingway to research the local bars. When the train pulled into Sudbury, he headed to the nearest beer hall to begin composing his dispatch. "In the dark it was impossible to tell much about the town except there were plenty of red-brick buildings, plenty of street lights, plenty of Chinese restaurants, and many girls on the street. There were movies showing Ben Turpin, French Canadian spoken in the bars, and real beer being sold on draft. I saw only three men drunk. In Cobalt there had been two men drunk at one bar before eleven in the morning."[11] After visiting the mine sites, Hemingway wrote a long piece that, while not debunking the British Colonial Coal claims, cast enough doubt on the operation to make any sane investor wary.

His only reward was a single evening off, but Hemingway made sure it was profitable. He and

Hadley took the streetcar to the Woodbine race-track. Using his wife's pregnant state as inspiration, Ernest put his money on a longshot named My Dear, which handily won the first race. He rein-vested the pot, at long odds, on a horse in the third called Baby Mine, which also galloped to victory, earning Ernest and Hadley $225. The winnings on that single evening, he wrote Ezra Pound, had seen him "making altogether about forty dollars more than I make in two weeks of eighteen hours a day of toil. It has destroyed whatever pleasure I get from dragging down the pay envelope. Thus are we buggered by destiny, as Hamlet remarked."[12]

CHAPTER 10

Disgrace Under Pressure

WHILE IN TORONTO, HEMINGWAY AND HADLEY BOTH ENJOYED playing the role of Left Bank intellectuals to the hilt. They adopted a bohemian style of dress and appearance: Ernest wore a French beret and faded sports shirt with no tie and muddy workboots; Hadley dressed in plain and simple clothing, had a short, boyish haircut and wore no makeup or jewelry. Simply by virtue of his unconventional appearance, Hemingway would be noticed when he entered the newsroom. However, not everyone was convinced that he was an artist. Most of the reporters had read his Paris dispatches, his interviews with world leaders, his gripping account of the evacuation of Constantinople, but it was really only the younger and more literate ones who felt he was a burgeoning writer of fiction. During one late shift, deskman Jimmy Cowan had slipped a copy of *Three Stories & Ten Poems* to Morley Callaghan. After reading the collection, the enthusiastic cub reporter discussed it with two of the more senior journalists, but they remained skeptical of Hemingway's talent:

> I couldn't resist asking [the older reporters] if they had read *Three Stories & Ten Poems*. They had. And what did they think of it? Their supercilious contempt enraged me. When I argued with them, they dismissed me good-humoredly. After all, they didn't even know my name. I can still remember the patient smile of the older one as he said, "Remember this, my boy, three swallows never made a summer."
>
> "All right. I think he's a great writer," I said belligerently. "Now just wait and see."[1]

Even such old friends as Greg Clark were not so sure about Hemingway's future as a fiction writer. Hemingway had modestly told Clark about his friendships with Ezra Pound, James Joyce and Gertrude Stein. One evening, when Ernest and Hadley were invited to the Clarks' for dinner, Hemingway wore his flowing Italian army cape in an attempt to indoctrinate Clark into the mystique of bullfighting. He turned the cape inside out to expose the red lining and demonstrated *veronicas* and other bullfighting techniques he had picked up the summer before in Pamplona. With each pass of the imaginary living-room bull, Hemingway gallantly executed a move and called out its proper name in bullfighting parlance. Bullfighting was more than a sport, he proclaimed, because it had all the elements of a classic tragedy. As he spoke, he liberally peppered his descriptions with as many Spanish words as he could remember, and referred to his new hero, the bullfighter Nicanor Villalta, who had impressed him with his bravery at the Pamplona fiesta only months ago.

All of Hemingway's dramatic performances were wasted. Clark would never become an aficionado of bullfighting or Spain. He preferred to stick with hunting and fishing in Ontario's northlands. But Hemingway's new love of all things Spanish could explain Greg Clark's recollection that Hemingway then had a speech impediment and sometimes could not pronounce the letter *L*. Clark later said that Hemingway could not properly say the name of the bullfighter Villalta, pronouncing it as "Vew-owa." However, this may have been simply a case of a young Hemingway showing off his new-found grasp of Spanish pronunciation, in which the dou-ble *L* is pronounced as a *Y*. If Clark did not understand this rule of Spanish, then Hemingway would indeed sound as though he had suddenly acquired a speech impediment. Clark's only other reference to Hemingway's impediment was his pronunciation of the word "Itaw-yan" (see pg. 50), but this could have been a misunderstanding of Hemingway's over-dramatic foreign pronunciation.

Later, Hemingway presented a signed copy of *Ten Stories & Three Poems* to Clark and stood shyly, weaving and nervously shadowboxing, as he awaited a verdict. After reading the collection, Clark still insisted that Ernest's true talent was as a feature writer. "It stinks," Clark offered bluntly. "You see, it's bumpy. What you gotta do in order to be a great feature writer on *The Star Weekly* is write nice and smooth, you see, and sort of flow your language on. Don't *hammer* it on, for God's sake."[2]

From that moment on, Callaghan recalled, Hemingway began using Greg Clark's opinion as a reverse barometer of quality. If Clark liked a piece of fiction, Hemingway tore it up. But if Clark really and truly hated a short story, Ernest was convinced that he had created a work of true and lasting literary value.

*Ernest and Hadley found a tiny apartment in the
Cedarvale Mansions building at 1599 Bathurst
Street, on the northern limits of the city. A balcony at
the rear looked out over miles of open countryside.*
(*Toronto Star* photo)

After staying three weeks in the Selby Hotel, the Hemingways managed to find a small apartment in a new building called Cedarvale Mansions at 1599 Bathurst Street, close to the Connable home. Despite its name, the Cedarvale building was no mansion. The apartment was nothing more than a small rectangular room with a Murphy bed and a balcony overlooking a ravine. It wasn't much, but, as Hemingway noted in an unpublished sketch, the balcony at least offered a feeling of space. The view, he wrote, "is very fine. All the trees are changing colors and beyond the ravine you can see the open country."[3] The Hemingways signed a one-year lease and were to move in on Saturday, September 29. But when moving day arrived, Hemingway was once again sent out of town on assignment, leaving Hadley to move the furniture and boxes that had arrived from Chicago and St. Louis up four flights of stairs, with help from friends and an elderly janitor.

Hadley decorated the apartment with paintings Ernest had bought in Paris, including works by André Masson, Dorothy Shakespear and Kumae. Ernest's father sent a crate containing china and crystal. There was a white rocking chair, a bathtub standing on claw feet and, dominating the cramped space, a rented grand piano for Hadley. They adopted a cat, which they soon discovered was not house-trained. In a letter to Pound, Hemingway noted that the cat had made a "shitting place" behind the bathtub. "Later in the evening, I will track down this piece of merde by its smell and will carefully wipe it up with the aid of a copy of the *Toronto Star*."[4]

So small was the apartment that, when the Murphy bed was pulled down from the wall, it blocked the way to the balcony. One night, as Hadley, nearly nine months pregnant, lay sleeping, Hemingway returned home with Ernest Smith and another friend. They had been drinking and, since Hemingway had a fresh bottle of whisky, were clearly not yet ready to call it a night. Hemingway climbed over sleeping Hadley to the balcony and then instructed his friends to do the same. Smith was halfway over the bed, crawling over Hadley's legs, when she suddenly woke up. Formal introductions were made all round as Smith and the other friend climbed over Hadley.

During this period of their stay in Toronto, Hemingway would often appear moody and depressed when he returned from work. He could not bring himself to write fiction of any kind while confined in such a small living space and with such a demanding job. Hadley was beginning to recognize that the return to Toronto had probably been a mistake. "Ernest is distracted by the job which is run on the most crazy, uneconomical principles and is also greatly overworked," she wrote to Ernest's parents. "So many trips, no sleep, and countless unimportant assignments."[5]

Early in October, with Hadley due to give birth any day, Hindmarsh suddenly sent Hemingway to New York City to cover the North American visit of David Lloyd George. The assignment was a tall order. Hemingway was first to meet with the former British prime minister and his daughter Megan in New York and then to ride with them on a special train that would tour Canada. With so many citizens of British descent in Toronto, the *Star* wanted blanket coverage of the event, and had originally planned to send feature writers Mary Lowrey and Robert Reade along with Hemingway. But when Ernest boarded the train, he was all alone. At the last moment Hindmarsh had decided that the young journalist should handle the assignment by himself.

After listening to the bombastic (and in Hemingway's mind, extremely silly) speech of welcome from New York's Deputy Mayor Hulbert, Hemingway followed George throughout the day, covering his speech at a United Press luncheon at the Biltmore Hotel and at two more press conferences in the afternoon. He even tailed George and his wife and daughter to the Music Box Theatre that evening to see how they would react to Irving Berlin's new *Music Box Revue*. At the theatre, a mob of Irish Republican sympathizers threw eggs at George but missed him and hit bystanders. Hemingway got it all down, reporting every detail, no matter how insignificant, to show Hindmarsh that he was capable of covering a big story. No event that unfolded, no comment that was made — apart from the deputy mayor's ridiculous speech — was deemed unworthy of inclusion in his dispatches.

That first day alone, Hemingway was on the job for nineteen hours straight. He filed ten stories in four days; eight of these were published and two others — a first-person account of following George as he played a round of golf and another about how George was "the Great Survivor" — were spiked by *Star* editors. (See Appendices 16 and 17.)

In his few spare moments in New York, Hemingway tried, unsuccessfully, to contact Sherwood Anderson. He also visited a number of bookstores, and from one bought a copy of the journal *Little Review*. In it were published six of his vignettes from *in our time*, as well as his poem "They All Made Peace," which lampooned the pompous world leaders he had interviewed while covering the Lausanne conference for the *Star* in 1922. This poem, which appeared next to a work by Gertrude

Stein, made Hemingway all the more homesick for the freedom of the literary life in Paris. In a letter to Stein, he writes the following description of New York. The city was clearly no substitute for Paris.

> New York looked very beautiful in the lower part around Broad and Wall streets where there is never any light gets down except streaks and the damndest looking people. All the time I was there I never saw anybody even grin. There was a man drawing on the street in front of the Stock Exchange with yellow and red chalk and shouting, "He sent his only begotten son to do this. He sent his only begotten son to die on the tree. He sent his only begotten son to hang there and die." A big crowd standing around listening. . . . "Pretty tough on de boy," said a messenger boy absolutely seriously to another kid. Very fine. There are really some fine buildings. New ones. Not any with names that we've ever heard of. Funny shapes. Three hundred years from now people will come from all over Europe and tour it in rubber neck wagons. Dead and deserted like Egypt. It'll be Cook's most popular tour.[6]

Although he did his best to fulfill the assignment, Hemingway's heart wasn't in it. He disliked Lloyd George and cynically believed the entire tour was a farce designed to land a rich American husband for daughter Megan. George was "a cantankerous, mean, temperamental and vicious man who never shows it in pooblic," he wrote to Stein. "He doesn't have all that long hair for nothing. Every night he cancels all his engagements for the next night and every morning wakes feeling chipper and damns his secretary for cancelling them. I have heard him at his best. He wants to make a fine marriage for Megan and hopes to re-launch himself on this side of the Atlantic."[7]

Hemingway, exhausted from overwork, also bitterly resented being sent out of town when his wife was due to give birth. In a letter that arrived at his hotel, Hadley reported that the apartment was starting to look homey now that a trunk had arrived from Oak Park full of Ernest's belongings and even some stored wedding presents. She had been reading his flurry of stories in the newspaper. "Articles grand," she wrote. "Love my Bubby and will smooch with him so joyously come Wedens tag morgen."[8]

Although Hemingway had been prolific in filing his dispatches, and had reported on George's every move, the one speech he decided not to report proved to be the most important in the *Star's* eyes.

Deputy Mayor Hulbert, a former lawyer and congressman, had a reputation as a verbose windbag who boasted of his country's greatness in the style of a circus spell-binder. His welcoming speech proved Hulbert was worthy of the reputation, as this sample sentence illustrates:

> If, as a new star risen in the east, there may arise a happy confederation of the people of Europe — such as your observations will disclose exists among the one hundred and ten million many-racialed inhabitants of the forty-eight states of the American union — if these peoples will join together in harmony and agreements on paths of peaceful pursuits, guided by the experience of the little group of struggling colonies which have become the most puissant of nations, then will the wheels of rehabilitation hum merrily, and then will world peace become a surety, and then will the millions of industrious men and women, sick unto death of strife and war, misery and grief, united in a song of praise for their deliverance, and, as one voice, will their paean of gratitude ascend to the throne of the Almighty God.[9]

Hulbert went on to thump his chest about how

glorious and forever-enduring was the American style of government, a system that had eradicated the aristocracy of old world nations and was "the best which God in His wisdom had ever vouchsafed for His children." When Lloyd George finally got a chance to respond with a speech of his own, he replied that he agreed with Hulbert's picture of modern America, "a picture which has sunk even into the European mind . . . slow as we, suffering from senile decay, with our arteries hardened by centuries of pretty hard work." George smiled as the press corps laughed at what they took to be a deliberate spoof of Hulbert's bombastic style. With what others reported as "a twinkle in his eye," George concluded by begging, "Don't be too hard on the old continent — I *come* from there."[10]

Hemingway, like many of the assembled reporters, thought Hulbert's speech was too silly to bother reporting. But the *New York Herald*'s reporter thought otherwise and filed a story stating that Hulbert had insulted Lloyd George by making remarks that disparaged Great Britain. Of course any insult to Britain was an insult to the readers of the *Toronto Star*. When *Star* publisher Joseph Atkinson read of Hulbert's speech in the *Herald*, he placed an angry call to Hindmarsh, wanting to know why the *Star* had been scooped on such a big story. He demanded that Hemingway be yanked off the Lloyd George tour at once and ordered back to Toronto to answer for his mistake.

But the call was too late. It was placed on Tuesday, October 9, and by then Hemingway was already heading back to Toronto, trading drinks, jokes and smutty stories with reporters aboard the press car of Lloyd George's special train, unaware that his exhausting, single-handed coverage of the tour had been viewed as a shocking failure and that he was coming home in disgrace.

On that same night, Hadley felt too ill and depressed to be left alone in the apartment. Since Ernest was not expected home for two more days, Hadley telephoned Harriet Connable and was told to come over at once. After dinner, Hadley, Dorothy and Harriet retired to the music room, and Hadley was told to sit back and relax as Harriet played the piano for her. Mrs. Connable played well, but her choice of music, including such maudlin numbers as "Auld Lang Syne," only deepened Hadley's sadness, and soon she was in tears. As the music played on, Hadley realized something else was causing her a very real and increasingly sharp pain. Mrs. Connable looked over as Hadley winced, and knew that something was wrong. "She asked if I was in pain," Hadley later wrote to a friend, "and of course I swore that I wasn't. But

I was beginning to. Finally, I said, 'Well, I really think something *is* happening.'"

They made it to the hospital at midnight. "We got there in the nick of time," Hadley recalled. "Of course, I missed Ernest terribly. He should have been there with me, suffering. I was laid out on a table, working away, pushing."[11] By two o'clock in the morning, a baby boy was born.

CHAPTER 11

Oh, Canada!

THE TRAIN WAS TEN MILES EAST OF TORONTO WHEN HEM-
ingway received news of the birth of his son. The
short message gave no indication of Hadley's condition, so he was more than anxious to see her,
to the extent that when a *Star* reporter met him
at Union Station and informed him that he was
to report to the city desk immediately, Hemingway
thrust his final notes on the Lloyd George visit
into his colleague's hands and raced out to hail
a cab to the hospital. Once there he "quite broke
down from fatigue and strain," Hadley wrote to
a friend, "and was as sweet as you and I know
he can be."[1]

The child was named John Hadley Nicanor, a
name that paid homage not only to Hadley but
also to John Hadley, Hemingway's favorite pen

*John Hadley Nicanor Hemingway was born in
Toronto's Western Hospital on October 10, 1923.
Hemingway missed the birth while on assignment
covering Lloyd George's arrival in New York.*
(John F. Kennedy Library)

name when double-dealing his newspaper work, as well as to the famous matador Nicanor Villalta. From early on, as could be expected of a couple who called each other Tiny and Wicky Poo, a pet name soon developed. The baby was nicknamed Mr. Bumby, which was soon shortened to simply Bumby. Hemingway was convinced that his son bore an uncanny resemblance to the King of Spain.

When he reported for work at the *Star* the day after returning from New York, Hemingway was immediately summoned to the assistant managing editor's office. Once behind closed doors, Hindmarsh pre-empted any angry words from Hemingway with a tirade of his own. He started out by blasting Ernest for going directly to the hospital without first reporting to the city desk and then bawled him out for getting scooped on the speech that had included statements that were insulting to British subjects.

In the bitter argument that followed, Hemingway told Hindmarsh that the Hulbert speech was silly, that he had gotten plenty of scoops for the *Star* and that he knew an important story when he saw one. As he later recapped the argument in a short-hand letter to Ezra Pound, "all work done by me from now on would be with the most utter contempt for [Hindmarsh] and all his bunch of masturbating mouthed associates. Also offered knock-down if editor's trap opened. Consequently, position at office highly insecure."[2]

Hemingway and Hadley began to make plans for him to quit the *Star* and together return to Paris as soon as possible. Hadley wrote to a friend to say how miserable they were at a time when they should be so happy and reported how Ernest had been "bawled out by that brute at the office for having come to me instead of taking the material to the office himself. It will kill my Tiny if we stay too long. He is almost crazy . . . staying is hell."[3]

When not at work, Hemingway suffered from insomnia, he also was losing weight and could not keep food down, as his stomach was shot from what he called "nervous fatigue." He began planning a novel called "The Son-In-Law," which would skewer Hindmarsh, the son-in-law of the *Star* publisher.

Ezra Pound had been urging Hemingway to send him his latest poems or works of fiction. Hemingway complained to Pound that any creative writing was impossible under the circumstances. He felt as though he were under constant fire once again, as he had been in the trenches of Italy. "Things are getting worse here. I am now undertaking the show on a day by day basis. Get through today. Then get through tomorrow, tomorrow. Like

1918. It is not, however, how to spend one of the few remaining years of one's life." Hemingway told Pound he was planning a rant against his adopted home called "Oh Canada," but the words would not come. "There is no doubt about [Canada] being the fistulated asshole of the father of seven among Nations. . . . Feel that I'm so full of hate and so damned, bitchingly, sickeningly tired that anything I do will be of little value. Still, the diseased oyster shits the finest pearls."[4]

Hindmarsh continued to exasperate him by pointing out his shortcomings as a reporter. After Hemingway failed to get a one-on-one interview with coal baron Sir Henry Thorton, Hindmarsh drove the point home with a memo that indicated that the hot-shot European reporter had once again been scooped by the competition. "I notice the *Globe* managed to get a good interview with Thorton," Hindmarsh's memo stated. "I think we should have stayed with him until we got him, as a personal interview yields a lot of color in addition to the subject matter."[5] Such primers on the basic elements of journalism served only to further anger and frustrate Hemingway. For who knew better than he how to write a colorful first-person interview? His 1922 Clemenceau interview — albeit rejected by the *Star* — was a classic example of a "color" personality profile. If Hemingway was good at one thing, it was descriptive detail — sometimes to a fault. In another memo, Hindmarsh offered more elementary advice: "I notice that Sir Henry Thorton is coming to Toronto on November 5th. . . . It is highly important that we secure a good article from him this time and it would be advisable for you to start now to prepare the subject and frame questions to put to him."[6]

The final straw between Hemingway and Hindmarsh was the Count Apponyi incident. Hemingway had had breakfast with the count, a seventy-seven-year-old Hungarian diplomat, who gave him the details of a speech he was to deliver that day at a city club. The count had shown Hemingway documents that laid out details of a League of Nations loan of a quarter of a million British pounds to Hungary, which was on the brink of financial ruin in the aftermath of the Great War, and Hemingway had asked if he could borrow the documents to help him write a story about the loan. The count was reluctant to part with the papers, which were the originals, but eventually agreed to lend them to Hemingway on the strict condition that they be safeguarded at all costs and returned as quickly as possible. Hemingway gave his word.

He filed his story, headlined "Hungarian Count Delighted with Loan," for the October 15, 1923, edition of the *Daily Star*, sending it by messenger to Hindmarsh, along with the borrowed documents as evidence of the importance of the loan to the stricken country. In a note appended to the documents, Hemingway stressed how important the papers were and asked Hindmarsh to put them in the office safe after reading them. Hindmarsh perused the documents but did not lock them away. Instead, they somehow ended up in his wastebasket. By the time Hemingway returned to the office to collect the papers, they had been taken away with the rest of the garbage and burned in the incinerator.

Hemingway was furious. Hindmarsh had not only made a fool of him but caused him to violate his word of honor. Was it an honest mistake on Hindmarsh's part, or was it just another tactic to humiliate and exasperate the "prima donna"?

After his blowup with Hindmarsh, Hemingway wrote almost exclusively for the *Star Weekly*. Hindmarsh had decided that Hemingway was not cut out to be a reporter on the *Daily* and recommended that he take most of his future assignments from J.H. Cranston, the *Star Weekly* editor who had given the young reporter first break back in the winter of 1920. Cranston not only welcomed his old protégé back into the *Weekly* fold but privately agreed on a side deal. "He came to see me, said he had decided to go back to Paris," Cranston later revealed, "and asked if he could write a series of articles for the *Star Weekly* in return for sufficient money to buy his rail and steamship tickets."[7] With the blessing of managing editor John Bone — who, like Cranston, was having his own difficulties with Hindmarsh — the agreement was struck. Hemingway would write for the *Weekly* to justify his *Star* salary and collect extra pay for any stories written above and beyond the call of duty. His output was so great that several of his later *Weekly* stories had to be published under pen names such as Peter Jackson in order to avoid the impression that he was writing almost the entire issue single-handedly.

This arrangement was, of course, much better for Hemingway. The *Weekly* staff worked at a more leisurely pace than the harried reporters in the city pool. And Hemingway, as before, was allowed a free rein in choosing subjects for his weekend-magazine features. It is not surprising that, by mid-October of 1923, the subject that was crowding his mind was Europe: in particular, France, Spain and Germany. The stories, most of which are collected in *Dateline, Toronto*, started spilling out. He wrote of trout fishing in Europe and game shooting in Europe, finding the most tenuous of local angles to allow him to launch into his reminiscing (the headline for the hunting article was "More Game to Shoot in Crowded Europe Than in Ontario"). He wrote about the "sordid" champagne-and-jazz nightlife of Paris, but reassured his readers that this "disease" was not so "altogether revolting," not so "disgusting, heavy, dull and hopeless" as the cabaret scene in Berlin, where cocaine could be found in abundance. And nowhere, of course, was as bad as Constantinople. Hemingway certainly knew how to give the puritans of Toronto what they wanted to hear. Such sensational reports, however, must have led some readers to wonder how he had acquired so much firsthand experience of the moral hell-holes of Europe.

Hemingway also wrote of avalanches in Switzerland and the gargoyles of Notre Dame and even used an anecdote about a crooked currency seller in Toronto's slum-like Ward as the peg on which to hang a story about the dubious worth of the German mark. When William Butler Yeats was awarded the Nobel Prize for literature in the autumn of 1923, Hemingway started a story by supposing that the average Toronto "club woman" would be surprised to learn that Yeats was not long dead. This gave him the chance to offer another thousand words or so of his opinion on the state of literature, complaining that no American author has yet won the coveted prize. (The honor would fall to Hemingway himself in thirty years to come.)

"It has just occurred to me," he writes, "that the Nobel committee don't read English very well." The Yeats story also offers one of the first indications that Hemingway was turning sour on his friend and benefactor Sherwood Anderson; he opines that Anderson had once seemed on a sure course to win the award "but he has swerved a long way off now."[8] Within three years, Hemingway would be savagely lampooning Anderson's book *Dark Laughter* in his first novel, *The Torrents of Spring*.

Hemingway even contributed a bit of disingenuous doggerel called "I Like Canadians," which told how "nice" Canadians were. If Hemingway's readers made the mistake of being flattered, it was fortunate that they could not read what he was saying about them in his never-ending flow of letters to literary friends in Paris. To Sylvia Beach, owner of the Shakespeare & Company bookstore in Paris, he wrote: "Canadians are all tapettes [gasbags] at heart underneath all the big free open spaces. There are no gigolos because no old women have money. Otherwise they would all be. It is a dreadful country. . . . We are the only nice people in Canada. . . . I would like to swing a crochet on the mention of Canada. I would like to hit Canada a coup bas [low blow]."[9] To Gertrude Stein and Alice B. Toklas he complained that the rent was too high and the beer too expensive. "What bothers me is that, with my fine intelligence, I ever came out here. . . . I am going to chuck journalism I think. You ruined me as a journalist last winter."[10]

It was during this *Star Weekly* period that Hemingway finally got around to writing his first two accounts of bullfighting in Spain (see Chapter 8). He had visited the annual Feria in Pamplona the previous July. "That was just three months ago," he writes at the end of his second feature, published on October 27, under the headline "World Series of Bull Fighting a Mad, Whirling Carnival." "It seems in a different century now, working in an office. It is a very long way from the sunbaked town of Pamplona where the men race through the streets in the mornings ahead of the bulls, to the morning ride to work on the Bay-Caledonia car. But it is only fourteen days by water to Spain. . . . There is always that room at 5 Calle de Eslava, and a son, if he is to redeem the family reputation as a bullfighter, must start very early."

CHAPTER 12

A Legend in the Making

WHILE ERNEST HEMINGWAY WAS CONTENDING WITH HIND-marsh in Toronto, elsewhere the literary world was beginning to take notice of him. In early November, Gertrude Stein sent him a copy of her review of his privately printed *Three Stories & Ten Poems*. The review, which was somewhat mixed in that it suggested he give up prose and stick to verse, was to appear in the November 27, 1923, edition of the *Paris Tribune*.

> *Three Stories and Ten Poems* is very pleasantly said. So far so good, further than that, and as far as that. I may say of Ernest Hemingway that as he sticks to poetry and intelligence it is both poetry and intelligent. Rosevelt [*sic*] is genuinely felt as young as Hemingway and as old as Rosevelt. I should say that Hemingway

should stick to poetry and intelligence and eschew the hotter emotions and the more turgid vision. Intelligence and a great deal of it is a good thing to use when you have it, it's all for the best.

Ernest knew that Stein thought the explicit sexuality of stories such as "Up in Michigan" was "turgid." She had not only told him to "start again and concentrate" but had also implied that this particular story was unpublishable.[1] Altogether the review was not exactly a rave, but it was his first, and Hemingway wrote to Stein to thank her for it.

Although Hemingway's journalistic work allowed him little time to devote to his fiction, he spent every spare moment working on the page proofs for *in our time*, the collection of his cablese vignettes that would be published in December 1923 by William Bird's Three Mountains Press in Paris. Many of the sketches were fictionalizations of stories he had written for the *Star*, for example his piece on the retreat of the refugees from Constantinople. Like *Three Stories & Ten Poems*, this new book would be slim, even after it was padded out with four blank pages at front and back, but it would be the first work to highlight Hemingway's hard, athletic prose style.

On December 3, Ezra Pound wrote a letter addressed to "Ernest Hemingway, Tomato, Can." telling of a new literary magazine, the *Transatlantic Review*, which was being started by Ford Madox Ford. Pound prodded Hemingway for the promised manuscript of his story "Oh Canada" as a submission to the review: "WHHHHHHHHHere's your copy? Wot's the use your pore old grandpa Ford sittin in a dammap cottage sweating 'is nek off to perduce a revoo where the Young can EXPRESS 'emselves IF you aren't goin ter com across wif de PUNCH? I think, meself, you'd better come bak here and direk the policy of the damn thing."[2] Unfortunately Hemingway did not have any copy to offer Pound. His frustration at being unable to write fiction while at the *Star* added to his rage over Hadley's negligence in losing his suitcase of stories in Paris. He had become moody and depressed in Toronto, and in any quarrel with his wife he had a ready ace in the hole to whip out: she had betrayed him by losing his stories just when things were starting to happen. "The fact that she had been so careless with his most precious possession [and] had shown so little understanding of his life as a writer dealt the first disastrous blow to their marriage," concluded biographer Jeffrey Meyers." The loss was irrevocably connected in Hemingway's mind with sexual infidelity, and he equated the lost manuscripts with lost love. He tried to forgive her, but he could not."[3]

Earlier that year, in Paris, American editor and writer Edward O'Brien had heard Ernest's tales of woe over his lost suitcase of manuscripts and had offered to publish one of the salvaged stories, the racetrack yarn "My Old Man," in the upcoming compendium *Best Short Stories of 1923*. In November of 1923, O'Brien wrote both to confirm that "My Old Man" was in the new collection and to ask if the volume could be dedicated to Hemingway. Hemingway wrote back: "Your letter couldn't have had a greater effect if it had been to inform me that I'd just been given 1 million dollars, the V.C., a renewable annual pass entitling self and family to the royal suite on The Mauretainia — with the promise that I would only have to make one more crossing. . . . Yes, you may dedicate the book to me."[4]

O'Brien did so (and misspelled Hemingway's name in the process). In his November letter, he had also asked Hemingway if he had enough new material to make up a collected works. Hemingway told him of the upcoming publication of *in our time* and added that, in Toronto and while working for the *Star*, he had not been able to turn out much new fiction. "Have felt pretty low and discouraged here," he told O'Brien. "Working so that you're too tired at night to think let alone write and then in the morning a story starts in your head on the street car and have to choke it off because it was coming so perfectly and easily and clear and right and you know that if you let it go on it will be finished and gone and you'd never be able to write it. I'm all constipated up inside with stuff to write, that I've got to write it before it goes bad in me."[5]

It was impossible to be literary in a "busted boom country" like Canada, Hemingway complained. How could you turn out heavenly works in a place that had "pretty much gone to hell"?

In the midst of his battle with Hindmarsh, two people at the *Star* whom Hemingway eventually came to confide in were Mary Lowrey and Morley Callaghan.

Lowrey, one of the few female *Star* reporters, had suffered the "Hindmarsh treatment" herself. When the newsroom pressure got to be too much for Hemingway, he often took refuge in her small office. "He would storm in there," Lowrey later said, "and rave and rant about so and so." Hemingway, with his usual knack for exaggeration, told Lowrey that his three months back in Toronto had cost him ten years of his literary career. He was so proud of his fiction, Lowrey recalled, that when the proofs for *in our time* arrived in Toronto in October, he brought them into the newsroom, telling whoever would listen that he had "invented a new style of writing." Occasionally, Hemingway joined Lowrey and other reporters as they met between assignments at Child's restaurant. Later, he took them to Angelos, on Elm Street, where he had made friends with the waiters who served wine in teacups to circumvent Toronto's liquor laws. There Hemingway showed off his knowledge of Italian and demonstrated how real Italians dunked their bread in wine. "Hemingway," Lowrey later said, "was always lots of fun."[6]

Callaghan had heard many magnified and conflicting stories about Hemingway before he finally had the opportunity to meet the man. He had heard about both the ongoing war with Hindmarsh and Jimmy Cowan's praise of the young journalist's literary abilities. While Callaghan was working in the *Star* library one day he suddenly recognized Hemingway sitting across from him. As he later recalled, "There was a real sweetness in his smile and a wonderful availability, and he made me feel that he was eagerly and deeply involved in everything."[7]

Hemingway soon began to speak openly to the twenty-year-old reporter, telling him how he had come to Toronto with good expectations but now felt smothered, could not work here, wanted to go back to Paris. Hemingway then offered his analysis of the talents and abilities (or lack thereof) of the other reporters and editors on staff. For some he had the highest praise, but for others nothing but brutal contempt. His intensity suggested that he might be bothered by something more than the ordinary pressures of work, yet when Callaghan "looked at his warm, dark face with the restless eyes . . . [he] liked him more. Words came from him not in an eloquent flow but with a quiet, tense authority."

Hemingway then went on to proclaim the greatness of writers such as Joyce, Stendhal and Flaubert as if letting Callaghan in on a closely guarded secret, all the time keeping an intense eye contact.

When Hemingway learned that Callaghan also wrote fiction, he suggested that they meet in the library that Friday and compare works in progress. But when Friday came, Callaghan was dispatched on an assignment. The next time they met, Callaghan saw for the first time another side of Hemingway that he would soon know well:

The following Monday afternoon I passed Hemingway on the stairs. Wheeling suddenly, four steps above me, big and powerful, he growled, "You didn't bring that story down."

"No, I was busy."

"I see," he said, then rude and brutal he added, "I just wanted to see if you were another goddamed phony."[8]

Shocked by this outburst, Callaghan made sure he had a story with him the next time he went to the library. When Hemingway appeared, they exchanged material. Callaghan had only to read a few proof pages of *in our time* before he realized that, although the stories were nothing more than long paragraphs, "they were so polished they were like epigrams, each paragraph so vivid, clean and intense that the scene he was depicting seemed to dance before my eyes."[9]

After reading Callaghan's story, Hemingway pronounced that he was a "real writer" and encouraged Callaghan to keep on working, told him that he had the gift, that it was only a matter of time, and — most important — "Whatever you do, don't let anyone around here tell you anything."

From that first encounter on, Hemingway and Callaghan met regularly to talk about writing. Although there were many would-be writers on staff — those who talked about someday writing that

*Morley Callaghan, although only a twenty-year-old,
part-time cub reporter, became Hemingway's literary
confidante during the fall of 1923. After reading
Callaghan's short stories, Hemingway proclaimed
him a "real writer" and helped him become one of
Canada's best-known novelists.*
(Courtesy of the Morley Callaghan estate)

great novel — Callaghan recognized that Hemingway was unique. He was a dedicated artist whose writing was his religion, and a man who would let nothing, or nobody, stand in the way of achieving his goals. "A writer is like a priest," Hemingway once told Callaghan. "He has to have the same feeling about his work."[10]

Hemingway had to spend his days churning out newspaper copy that sapped him of all energy for writing fiction, and some assignments saw him wearing some highly unlikely hats: Hemingway the environmental reporter, Hemingway the classical music reviewer, Hemingway the sob sister. Most of the new stories gathered at the back of this book were written at this time, during the fall of 1923. They have not been identified as Hemingway's until now, thanks to the combination of the denial of a fair share of bylines by editor Hindmarsh and Hemingway's scheme to earn extra money by writing articles for the *Star* under assorted pen names.

One newly discovered story, headlined "Cars Slaying Toronto's Splendid Oak Trees" (see Appendix 19), appeared in the fall of 1923 under the byline Peter Jackson. This name has been confirmed as a Hemingway pseudonym; another Peter Jackson story is included among the stories reprinted in *Dateline, Toronto*. One need only hear the cadence of the words to know that it is Hemingway at work:

> A chill, cold wind blows over High Park. There is snow in the air.
>
> Other trees sway with the wind. The pines seem to enjoy it. But the oaks are sullen and rigid. Stripped of their leaves by the wind, they stand stiff and despairing looking against the sky. For the oaks are dying.
>
> They are dying because they cannot stand the city. And the city comes nearer and nearer all the time.
>
> Other trees are built to make compromises with the city. They have special defences against the attacks the city launches against them. But the oak is not built for compromises. It is like some animal of prehistoric times, built only for a certain environment. And when that environment is changed, it dies.[11]

In a story that appeared without a byline in the October 20 *Daily Star* (see Appendix 18), Hemingway traveled to the town of Newmarket, northeast of Toronto, to interview an elderly woman whose family had been living in a historic home for five generations. In the article, headlined "Fifth

Generation of Family Lives On Old Canadian Manor," Hemingway employs a fictional device he learned from Gertrude Stein: the repeated use of a word to create an internal, symbolic echo throughout the story. In the Red Ryan chase article (Appendix 14), the repeated word is *dark*. This time the word *dusk* recurs throughout to convey the sense of twilight surrounding the woman and her house:

> Inside the house is dusky . . . and before the nine-foot-wide fireplace in the dusk sat an old lady, the Mistress of the Manor. . . .
>
> It was quite dark now. Mrs. Dawson brought out some fruit cake carefully wrapped in oiled paper from the sideboard in the great, dusky dining room with the fireplace that could hold an entire sawlog. . . .
>
> "Enoch Rodgers was the carpenter," Mrs. Dawson said, her mind running back and trying to collect early, half-remembered details in the dusk. "I think that the bricks were burned on the Phillips farm."[12]

The echoing techniques Hemingway experiments with in human-interest features such as these would soon be employed in his short stories. A notable example is "Cat in the Rain":

Their room was on the second floor facing the sea. It also faced the public garden and the war monument. . . . Italians came from a long way off to look at the war monument. It was made of bronze and glistened in the rain. It was raining. The rain dripped from the palm trees. Water stood in pools on the gravel paths. The sea broke in a long line in the rain and slipped back to down the beach to come up and break again in a long line in the rain.[13]

The repeated use of the word "rain" adds emotional impact to a story that has very little in the way of narrative. "Very little happens in 'Cat in the Rain' . . . and yet the story conveys meanings which one would almost be ready, on the first reading, to swear did not exist," writes Hemingway scholar Scott Donaldson.[14]

Hemingway got so carried away with description in some news reports that the reader could be forgiven for wondering when he would ever get to the point of the story. In an article headlined "Tossed About on Land Like Ships in a Storm," which appeared in the *Star* on September 25, 1923, Hemingway and Mary Lowrey interview two women who had survived a terrible earthquake in Yokohama, Japan. In great detail, Hemingway describes the house and the clothing worn by the mother and the daughter and even goes so far as to construct imaginary conversations taking place between himself and the "girl reporter." The description is all very fine, but it takes Hemingway 516 words to get to the actual news story and first use the word *earthquake*.

In the winter of 1923, shortly before Christmas, Hemingway arrived at work one day to find that Hindmarsh had penciled him in to do something that almost every *Toronto Star* reporter has had to do at one time or another — and still has to do to this day: write a moving appeal for donations to the *Star*'s charity for children, the Santa Claus Fund. Under the headline "She Sacrifices Herself That Children May Live" (see Appendix 23), Hemingway tackles the assignment with unexpected gusto and writes a rather purple account of a deserted mother:

> She had worked until she had become a shadow. Her big eyes in sunken lids seemed to hold flame as they glowed from the pallid transparency of her thin face. Her lips were colorless. There was not a spare ounce of flesh on her nor a spare gill of blood in her veins. Her bones showed as knobs and hollows in her gaunt cheeks.

She was literally giving her body as a sacrifice for the children's sake.[15]

Perhaps Hemingway's enthusiasm for this story
was due to the fact that he was expecting Santa
Claus funds of his own — the *Star* Christmas
bonus that would allow him to pay for his passage
to France.

According to many former *Star* journalists, Hemingway also reviewed classical music for the paper,
but despite exhaustive searches by a number of
Hemingway scholars, including the *Star*'s William
McGeary, no review that appeared in the newspaper can be attributed to the young writer. However, among Hemingway's handwritten notes there
is a musical piece written for a radio broadcast.
In 1922, the *Star* launched a radio station, CFCA,
which became the first to feature regular radio pro-
gramming in Canada (and one of the first to do
so in the world). And, on at least one occasion,
Hemingway reviewed a Massey Hall performance
by the Toronto Symphony. His barely legible
handwritten review begins with the personal re-
minder, "Write up Massey Hall broadcast tonight."
He then confesses that he is not an expert. "The
reporter knows nothing about radio. . . . The set
however was as big as a kitchen, large and black
and covered with knobs." It made a sound "like

a giant cat purring." Hemingway then provides a blow-by-blow account of what he deemed a "perfectly conventional but excellent classical program." He describes how one concerto "mounted to a Tchaikovsky finish," although there was "nothing ethereal about the program, even if it came through the ether." Yet he admits, "If the reporter didn't like it, the audience did for the applause went on and on . . . until they got their encore." He later reports positively on the Bach portion of the program. It is clear that the story was intended for radio and not the newspaper, because it contains the circled statement: "This is C.F.C.A., The Daily Star, to Canada broadcasting."[16]

In later years, Hemingway would shy away from broadcasting of any type or recordings of his speeches or reading — but on at least this one occasion, he was Ernest Hemingway, radio reporter.

Although Hemingway had found a convert at the *Star* in young Morley Callaghan, he seems not to have been able to forgive his older colleagues for failing to recognize his artistry. The following unpublished sketch perhaps offers some hint of his frustration as he sat at a borrowed typewriter in the *Weekly* office one day in the late fall of 1923, listening to older reporters Greg Clark and Robert Reade talk:

> And so they talked. Then they talked some more. Down through the ages. There it goes boys. Listen to it. Reade is a Rhodes scholar with a cockney wife and sodomistic leanings. Greg is an ex-Major of infantry and a very good soldier. Neither of them knows a goddam thing about what he is talking about. Down through the ages. Oh shit. Shit on the ages. They are the highest paid guys on the staff. Therefore they don't have to work. . . . Reade and Clark sit around and talk. Talk is cheap. Work is cheaper. . . . Tomorrow they will argue on something else. I hope I will not be there but it does not make much difference. You cannot work very well in the Weekly office anyway. . . . I am happy because I have a little African fetish from Angola. It is very beautiful and gives me pleasure. It is much better than Legers drawings. Neither of them would look at it. They only like new ideas when they come out of *Vanity Fair* or some other place like that. They do not like the little Fetish. Jimmy [Frise] likes it. He is the only artist on the paper except me. Greg is only an artist about his baby

and the war. They are the only things he understands. He doesn't understand them. But he understands very well the beautiful things he made up about them.

Jimmy understands people and is the best fellow I know. He understands everything. Not always clearly but still it is understanding. He understood Hadley the first time he met her. He doesn't know he understands.

Bobby Reade is dry inside his head. Dry and futile. Very dry and very futile. He can do easy tricks with his mind. It is like a second rate act on a vaudeville turn. There is really nothing there.

Down through the ages. Why is it down through the ages? Down through the ages. Down and out through the ages. No not that. Down through the ages. Way down through the ages. Down on the ages. Go down on the ages. And the sages. Down down down through the ages. He rages at the ages. Down through the ages. That will be about enough of that.

Now to return to Greg.

I have not done Greg justice. Maybe I have hurt him. It would be cruel to hurt him but also difficult because he is not flat but round all around. He would be hard to hurt because he is well rounded. He loves his wife and his baby. He loves hunting and fishing and his fishing tackle. He loves guns and books about guns. All of these are defences. It is easy to hurt a man who loves guns but not if he knows he can always go hunting. He loves to think. He thinks very well but he never strains himself. He likes it about Canada too. What I dislike he dislikes too but it does not touch him. He is not afraid of other people. He is very sympathetic and he will always listen. He really listens. He understands words and ideas and conditions and emergencies and courses of conduct. He understands religions and governments. Jimmy understands none of these but he understands what is under them all. Greg is very romantic. He is very fine but I can never understand all the way inside of him because he is romantic. I am romantic too and that is the trouble. You cannot dismiss him or classify him because he is always acting and you cannot tell how much of it is acting. He also acts inside himself. He is an officer and a gentleman. It is better that way.

He does things for people. He is honestly interested in people. There is too much India rubber in him. I have never seen him angry. He has too much sense. If he has a weakness it is having too much sense. He writes the best of anyone on the paper. I have known him a long time but I do not know much about him.

I do not know all about a man until I have seen him cry. Sooner or later you will see every man cry. It is like chemistry. When he cries is when he is separated into his component parts. Greg is my friend and I know less about him than I do about Hindmarsh. Hindmarsh is a son of a bitch and a liar and they are easy to understand. A good man is hard to understand. A son of a bitch always goes by the rules.

Jimmy I understand about. The only thing I hold against Greg is that he did not know it about horse racing or about boxing. They are the tests of a man. But I don't hold it against him. Besides I have never seen him drunk. I would like to see him drunk. I like to see every man drunk.

I would like to be drunk now.

I love getting drunk.

Right from the start it is the best feeling.[17]

Whether this was a typing finger-exercise or an attempted literary sketch is unclear. But it sheds some light on how Hemingway saw his *Star* colleagues — and himself — in the late fall of 1923.

Hemingway was not content to merely earn extra cash under the table by writing for the *Star Weekly* under assorted pen names. In November of 1923 — partly to pad his bank account but no doubt partly out of spite — Hemingway began secretly writing for two of the *Star*'s biggest rivals, the *Globe* and the *Mail and Empire*. Preserved in Hemingway's clipping scrapbook is an article headlined, "Moscow Theatre Company Will Not Come To Toronto," which appeared without a byline on the front of the *Globe*'s City News Section on November 27, 1923 (See Appendix 21). Hemingway had already proved himself capable of such journalistic infidelity by writing for two rival news services while in Europe as the *Star*'s foreign correspondent. But he was a full-time staff reporter for the *Star* at the time his *Globe* article appeared, and he knew that such double-dealing was the ultimate act of treason in the fiercely competitive newspaper world. If Hemingway's moonlighting had been discovered, he would have been fired on the spot. As a parting shot before he left Toronto, Hemingway wrote two articles, one headlined "Greatest Boy Actor Is a Toronto Lad" and the other "Marks Not Caused by Ill-Treatment," for the *Mail and Empire*. (See Appendices 24 and 25.) Whatever money he earned for the *Globe* and the *Mail and Empire* articles was likely of secondary importance. Hemingway was making a point, at least to himself: the *Star* did not own him. It was his way of thumbing his nose at this newspaper and especially at Hindmarsh.

CHAPTER 13

A Farewell to Toronto

THE DECISION TO RETURN TO PARIS HAD BEEN MADE IN EARLY November, but Hemingway did not formally announce that he was leaving the *Star* until December 26 — this way he was entitled to his Christmas bonus; his last day on the newspaper staff was January 1, 1924. However, the exact details of how he ended his tenure there — like so many other events in Hemingway's life — have been blown up into mythic proportions over the years.

There are at least four diverse accounts of how Hemingway quit the *Star*. One story that definitely has no basis in fact is the one in which Hemingway supposedly leaves Toronto in disgrace, fired by Hindmarsh "because he could not write."[1]

The best-known version of Hemingway's departure, now a newsroom legend, has it that he wrote a long tirade against Hindmarsh, venting his spleen on page after page of copy paper, which he then carefully pasted together and pinned to the bulletin board. This poison-pen letter of resignation is said to have been sixteen feet long, so long that it dragged and curled up on the floor below the bulletin board. Depending on which version is being told, the anti-Hindmarsh rant stayed on the board for anywhere from one to three days. Although Hindmarsh most certainly passed the notice board on his way in and out of the newsroom, he apparently refused to acknowledge it.

No record of this infamous notice remains, but from all accounts Hemingway was entirely capable of unleashing such a furious outburst. Real or imaginary, it is still the most legendary memo in the *Toronto Star*'s newsroom lore, and there are at least three explanations about when and why it was written.

One explanation is that Hemingway wrote it in October 1923 as a response to being "bawled out by the brute at the office" over the Lloyd George fiasco. Colleagues Greg Clark and Jimmy Cowan, who both remembered seeing the pasted-together screed, said it was definitely written in the aftermath of the New York trip: "[Hemingway was] furiously mad because he said . . . he thought he'd covered Lloyd George better than any of the American papers," Cowan recalled. "I was in the *Weekly* office alone with him that night, when that thing was up on the notice board. I thought he was [being] almost childish." After the note had been up for a day or so, Hemingway rather sheepishly decided to take it down himself. "He said to me, 'You know, I wonder if it'd be all right if I take that thing down off the notice board? I haven't kept a copy and I want to show it to my wife.' So he finally took it down off the board. . . . He didn't want to talk that night."[2]

Gordon Sinclair, who later became a famous *Star* reporter and broadcaster, was a copy boy for the newspaper when Hemingway returned to Toronto in 1923. His tale of Hemingway's resignation has been widely circulated, is often reprinted in newspapers and magazine stories and was even included in Denis Brian's *The True Gen*, a book of interviews that aims to strip away the falsehoods and get at the real story of Hemingway's life in the words of those who knew him. According to Sinclair, Hemingway quit shortly after the *Star* donated an elephant named Stella to Toronto's Riverdale Zoo. When the elephant promptly died at the zoo, it looked like a public relations disaster for the newspaper, but they were able to turn it into a promotional coup by announcing a contest in which Toronto children were invited to vote on what kind of animal should replace Stella as the *Star*'s gift to zoology. Although a wide assortment of beasts were suggested, Sinclair claimed that the paper had an angle on a white peacock at a reasonable price. In this way, the paper "conned" the children into choosing the bird. And Hemingway was assigned to welcome the peacock to Toronto and orchestrate a contest to find it a name. Being asked to do promotional work so enraged Hemingway that he quit on the spot after pinning the now infamous notice to the board. "It included the complaint that Hindmarsh treated him like dirt, overworked him and lied to him," Sinclair said. "The very first sentence was, as I remember it: 'I, Ernest Hemingway, will not now or ever write about any goddamn peacock.'"[3] Sinclair is the only one who has ever mentioned this incident.

Other accounts say Hemingway quit as a direct result of Hindmarsh's careless disposal of the official documents entrusted to Hemingway by Count Apponyi. The incident (which occurred shortly after the Lloyd George reprimand) appears to be the most probable cause of Hemingway's decision to quit. An undated and unsigned handwritten letter of resignation exists among Hemingway's papers. Whether this memo was ever typed and sent to managing editor John Bone is unknown, but it makes sense as a protest against Hindmarsh's negative reactions to his work on the Lloyd George and Count Apponyi stories. The reference to Hindmarsh making a "mistake" indicates that this was not written until after the second argument, over the discarded papers. The reference to a previous "long memorandum" lends credence to the story that Hemingway had earlier penned a long, angry memo after he and Hindmarsh had fought over the Lloyd George story.

Mr. Bone.

Before I came on the Star staff all my dealings had been with you. Since I joined the staff they have been with Mr. Hindmarsh.

Yesterday in the course of conversation with me Mr. Hindmarsh proved that he is neither a just man, a wise man, nor a very honest man. I have made every effort to get along with Mr. Hindmarsh. I do my work and have been kept busy with that.

But if work accomplished counts for nothing, nor results, and the only standard is to be at the mercy of any fit of temper or an outraged morbidity of dignity because of fancied slights. If it is a question of Mr. Hindmarsh or myself I of course must go. I was horrified while handling a big story, requiring speed and accuracy above all things, to be made the victim of an exhibition of wounded vanity from a man in a position of Assistant Managing Editor on a newspaper of the caliber of the Star because he himself had made a mistake.

There is something morbid about it. For some reason Mr. Hindmarsh *says* that I think I know more about assignments he gives me than he does. I have given him no cause to think this and I cannot be accused of every thot [sic] that his inferiority complex suggests to him.

I wrote you a long memorandum several days ago when Mr. Hindmarsh first began to try to force me into a quarrel. But I was so surprised at the way things were going that I could not believe it and put the memorandum away thinking Mr. Hindmarsh must be working under great pressure, and in no case desiring to go over his head.

I of course have the facts on the entire matter at your disposal. It is useless for me to continue to work on the Star under Mr. Hindmarsh.[4]

Whatever the reasons for Hemingway's departure from the *Star*, he waited until after Christmas before officially quitting. His official note of resignation, dated December 26, was terse and to the point:

> Mr. Bone:
>
> I regret very much the necessity of tendering my resignation from the local staff of the Star. This resignation to take effect January 1st, 1924, if convenient to you.
>
> Please believe there is no rudeness implied through the brevity of this memorandum.
>
> Ernest.[5]

Hemingway's carefully worded reference to quitting the "local staff" of the paper allowed him to keep his options open to contribute European dispatches from Paris. As it turned out, however, Hemingway never again had to rely on the *Star* as a source of income.

CHAPTER 14

Into the Sunrise,
1924

BEFORE HE LEFT FOR PARIS, HEMINGWAY MADE A QUICK PRE-Christmas trip to Oak Park to see his family. As usual, the visit was arranged to be as brief as possible: he was there less than a day. He caught a train on December 23 and was back in Toronto by Christmas Day in time to join Hadley for dinner at the Connables'. He would not have gone at all if his father had not paid for the trip. Dr. Hemingway had also offered round-trip tickets for Hadley and Bumby, but they were left behind on the excuse that such a whirlwind trip would be disruptive to the nursing of the child. This decision especially disappointed Hemingway's father; his chronic depression had worsened and he had hoped to be cheered by the sight of his daughter-in-law and new grandchild.

Hemingway poses with brother Leicester during a one-day visit to his Oak Park, Illinois, home on Christmas Eve 1923. Although his mother greeted him as a mature man who had found himself, within weeks she would be shocked by the "filth" of his second book, in our time. (John F. Kennedy Library)

Hemingway apparently had his own reasons for leaving Hadley and the baby behind. It seems that, despite any appearances to the contrary, he was going home not to renew his family ties but to sever them. On looking at her son, Grace Hemingway wept tears of joy after deciding that her "thoroughbred,"[1] as she called him, had at last found himself, had finally decided to settle down and make something of himself in life. Hemingway posed for photographs with his arm around his younger brother, Leicester, offering no hint that this was to be his last trip home. He was civil to his sister Marcelline, with whom he had so often fought. But before he left, he gave her a copy of *Three Stories & Ten Poems*. If she was flattered by this gift, the feeling soon turned to revulsion as she read the sexually explicit final scene of "Up in Michigan."

> One of Jim's hands went inside her dress and stroked over her breast and the other hand was in her lap. . . . Then the hand that felt so big in her lap went away and was on her leg and started to move up it. . . . The boards were very hard. Jim had her dress up and was trying to do something to her. She was frightened but she wanted it. She had to have it but it frightened her.[2]

The story made Marcelline feel ill, as Hemingway no doubt knew it would. Sex was a taboo subject in the Hemingway household. In Hemingway's autobiographical short story "Fathers and Sons," young Nick Adams reads that the tenor Enrico Caruso is a "masher" and asks his father what mashing means. The doctor will not answer directly, but assures his son that it is "one of the most heinous of crimes." He then offers a blanket condemnation of sex: "His father had summed up the whole matter by stating that masturbation produced blindness, insanity and death, while a man who went with prostitutes would contract hideous veneral diseases and that the thing to do was to keep your hands off of people."[3]

Hemingway did not grow up to become a masher, but he did take delight in rebelling against Oak Park's pious morals by writing graphic sex scenes that were calculated to shock prudes. Still, he was not yet ready to show his mother and father such material, and he did not even tell them about *Three Stories & Ten Poems*. But after he returned to Toronto, he mailed them an order form for his new book, *in our time*, which had just been published. Hemingway's father placed an order for six copies, thinking that it was his son's first book. As soon as he began reading it, however, he was disgusted and said he would not allow such "filth in the house";[4] he promptly returned all six copies to the Paris publisher. Hemingway would never forgive him for this.

On his last day on the job, January 1, 1924, Hemingway stopped by the *Star Weekly* office to visit Greg Clark, in the same cramped office that he had first entered as an unpublished writer four years earlier, the same office where he had once sat on a radiator and talked of his experiences only to be labeled as a phony and a "hanger-on" by Clark. As usual, Clark was in conversation with other senior reporters. Hemingway tried to discuss his dreams of a new kind of writing, but Clark still felt his younger friend was a fool to give up the chance to write features for the hottest paper in Canada. Hemingway said his farewells, and having heard of Ernest's ironic letter from Ezra Pound, his closest Toronto friends gave him a symbolic parting gift: a tomato can.

Earlier, Hemingway had taken Morley Callaghan aside and urged him to keep on writing. They had gone for a long walk up to the corner of Bloor and Bay Streets. As he loafed along, Hemingway had shadowboxed to punctuate his description of how Dostoyevsky wrote like a prize fighter, swarming all over you in a flurry of punches. In a little bookstore, Hemingway bought a copy of *Three Stories & Ten Poems* and autographed it for Callaghan.

Now, on Hemingway's last day at the *Star*, Callaghan dropped by to say goodbye. "I remember he was sitting with the three top writers of the *Star Weekly*," Callaghan later wrote. "Greg Clark, who was his friend, Charlie Vining and Fred Griffen. As I approached, these three men looked at me in surprise, for they didn't even know me." Callaghan was nervous as he walked up to shake hands. This was clearly a situation where a cub could be told to get lost. But to the shock of the older writers, Hemingway took the kid seriously. He told the part-time reporter to send any short stories he could produce to him in Paris, care of Guaranty Trust. He promised to spread the word. And then he said, "I'll see you in Paris."[5]

Before he could finally flee from Toronto, Hemingway had one more hurdle to overcome. He had to figure out how to break the one-year lease he had signed on his Bathurst Street apartment. He could not simply pack up and start moving out, or the landlord would have the police on him. So, as friends came to the apartment to say goodbye, Hemingway had each one carry out a single piece of furniture: a painting, a chair, a suitcase. In this way he and Hadley were able to empty the apartment unnoticed.

On January 9 he went out for a drink with Jimmy Cowan, who mentioned that he was planning to marry soon. On the spur of the moment, Ernest suggested that Cowan get married in the Hemingways' apartment. Three days later, Cowan and his bride-to-be, Grace Williams, walked up the stairs and into a bizarre scene. The apartment had been almost completely stripped of furnishings. Only the rented grand piano remained, with the infant Bumby tethered to a piano leg. Hemingway, the best man, had visited a bootlegger and laid in a supply of liquor. A clergyman was on hand, and seven others were invited to be part of the wedding party. When the clergyman pointed out that a witness would be required, Hemingway button-holed a bewildered neighbor for the task. After the ceremony, the neighbor, Jim Jackson, left without even being introduced to the bride and groom. The minister, who seemed extremely rattled by the setting, raced through the ceremony in record time and then, eyeing Hemingway's fresh supplies, let it be known that he was not averse to taking a drink.[6]

That evening, the Connables threw Ernest and Hadley a farewell party at the mansion. The next day, the Connable limousine picked up the Hemingways for a last ride down the hill to Union Station. Ernest Hemingway's four-year association with Toronto had come full circle, ending as it had begun, on a cold January day. Harriet Connable and Mary Lowrey saw them off on the sixteen-hour train trip to New York City.

On January 19, the Hemingways boarded the Cunard liner *Antonia*, bound for Cherbourg. The same day, his last article appeared in the *Star Weekly*, a tale of how some Toronto louts had mocked his hat as he rode on the streetcar. It was a floppy, felt green Alpine hat that he had purchased in Germany. Hemingway wrote what amounted to an obituary for his old "Freiburg Fedora" in his final words to appear in the *Toronto Star*:

> Since then the old hat seemed to have lost a little something in every country it had shed rain and wind and sun in. The hot sun of the Thracian desert had burned most of the green out of it, it had been chafed by heavy snow glasses strapped to it, and it had gained nothing by being sailed down into the sunbaked sand of the bullring.
>
> It was obviously a disreputable and, no doubt, funny-looking hat. So I folded it up and stuck it in my hip pocket and walked to the nearest hat store bare-headed.
>
> "What kind of hat do you want, sir?" asked the clerk, ignoring gracefully the fact that I was bare-headed.

After four months of the pious atmosphere of
"Toronto the Good," Hemingway made up for lost
time upon his return to Paris in January 1924.
(John F. Kennedy Library)

"Oh," I said, "give me one of the kind that everyone is wearing."

I have one of that kind now. But I know very
well that if I ever try to wear it in Europe, somebody
will want to take a poke at me.

As the *Antonia* slipped away from New York, Hemingway was already in an expatriate state of mind, turning heads as he strolled the decks in what one witness called "outlandish" knickerbockers, golf socks and a beret. He was happy to be heading back to Paris. Hadley did not relax, however, until the ship was well out at sea. She could not shake the fear "that the Canadian authorities would come aboard and take us off the ship for jumping the apartment lease."[7]

But Ernest knew that Toronto and daily journalism were safely behind him forever. He had learned much from journalism. "Hemingway's debt to journalism was a large one and he always acknowledged it," wrote biographer Charles Fenton. "The rather special pattern of Hemingway's employers [at the *Star Weekly*] had . . . permitted and encouraged the development of such an important instrument of his fiction as dialogue . . . and enabled Hemingway to exercise the lucid exposition which would in three years vivify *The Sun Also Rises*."[8]

Other reporters at the *Star* had been broken into harness, forced to kneel. But Hemingway would kneel only when in prayer, and writing was his only religion, and from now on he would have to write only the things he truly believed in. "Once you put a thing in words," he said, "unless you 'do it on your knees,' you kill it."[9]

Hemingway would always maintain that newspaper work had value for an aspiring writer "up to the point that it forcibly begins to destroy your memory" by forcing you to "forget every day what happened the day before. . . . A writer must leave [journalism] before that point. But he will always have scars from it."[10]

Hemingway had his own memories and his own scars as he left journalism and Toronto behind him forever. But he knew the time was right as the *Antonia* steamed east toward the horizon with the sun about to rise.

A Man of the World

ERNEST HEMINGWAY'S LITERARY CAREER BLOSSOMED IN PARIS. He signed a three-book deal with New York publishers Boni & Liveright, and in 1925 his first trade book, *In Our Time*, was published, containing fourteen short stories and the vignettes from *in our time*. Hemingway felt that Boni & Liveright did not push the book, and it angered him that they printed only 1,300 copies. That same year he befriended F. Scott Fitzgerald, who urged him to send a novel he was writing about bullfighting in Spain and Paris bohemian life to Fitzgerald's editor, Max Perkins, at Charles Scribner and Sons in New York. Yet Hemingway could not get out of his deal with Boni & Liveright unless they rejected his second book, which was to be a novel. Boni & Liveright had just published *Dark Laughter*, by Sherwood

Anderson, their best-known author. Hemingway, determined to break his contract, used his considerable gifts as a humorist to write, in a ten-day binge, *The Torrents of Spring*, a vicious parody mocking Anderson's style and his "dear reader" interjections. He made up the story as he went along, and if interrupted, simply included the source of the interruption in the story, as he did the day Fitzgerald showed up at his apartment in a drunken stupor and would not leave.

> It was at this point in the story, reader, that Mr. F. Scott Fitzgerald came to our home one afternoon, and after remaining for quite a while suddenly sat down in the fireplace and would not (or was it could not, reader?) get up and let the fire burn something else so as to keep the room warm. I know, reader, that these things sometimes do not show in a story, but, just the same, they are happening, and think what it means to chaps like you and me in the literary game.[1]

Boni & Liveright rejected *The Torrents of Spring*, and, with the contract broken, it was published by Scribner's in 1926. Later that year, *The Sun Also Rises* was published by Scribner's. It was Hemingway's second novel, but his first real one. Almost overnight, he became an internationally famous author and was recognized as a spokesman for the "Lost Generation." The book sold well, was highly acclaimed by critics and was labeled "one of the filthiest books of the year" by Grace Hemingway.[2] Ernest Hemingway had arrived.

In 1925, Ernest fell in love with Pauline Pfeiffer, one of Hadley's best friends. After a year of agonizing indecision, he and Hadley were divorced. It was a decision Hemingway would forever be haunted by; he later said, "I wished I had died before I ever loved anyone but her."[3] Hadley's biographer, Giola Diliberto, writes that Hadley "recovered from the desertion and went on to lead a cheery, if somewhat tipsy, life as the wife of newspaperman and poet Paul Scott Mowrer. Like the characters in a Hemingway story, they spent a lot of time fishing and drinking."[4] Hadley died in 1979, aged eighty-seven.

John "Bumby" Hemingway is a well-known sportsman. He lives in Ketchum, Idaho, and is the father of actresses Margaux and Mariel Hemingway and the artist Joan Hemingway.

Dr. Clarence Hemingway, suffering from severe depression, committed suicide in 1928. On Ernest's request, Grace mailed him the gun his father had used.

Grace Hemingway died in 1951. Two days after

John "Bumby" Hemingway, pictured here at a young age, is father of actresses, Margaux and Mariel Hemingway. (John F. Kennedy Library)

his mother's death, Hemingway wrote to biographer Carlos Baker to say that her passing had conjured memories of how beautiful she had been and how happy his childhood had been "before everything went to hell in the family."[5]

Greg Clark and Jimmy Frise quit the *Star* in 1946, moving as a team to a rival weekend magazine, the *Montreal Standard*. Because Hindmarsh had a reputation for firing reporters on Christmas Eve (to avoid having to pay them a Christmas bonus), Clark and Frise both dated their resignation letters December 24. Two years later, Frise died of a heart attack. Clark continued to write his humor and outdoors columns, many of which have been collected in book form. But despite the advice he handed out to Hemingway, Clark never did fulfill his own secret ambition to write a novel. He died in 1977, at eighty-five.

Managing editor John Bone died of a heart attack while at work in his office on June 7, 1928. Harry Hindmarsh became managing editor of the *Star*, and in 1932 made himself managing editor of the *Star Weekly* as well. Although *Star Weekly* editor J. Herbert Cranston had worked at the paper for twenty-nine years, Hindmarsh offered him only two choices: he could take a 50 percent cut in pay and accept a demotion to city desk copy editor, or he could resign. Cranston resigned. He later became editor of a small weekly paper in Midland, Ontario. In 1951, a year before Cranston died, Hemingway wrote him to say, "I never enjoyed myself so much as working under you and with Greg Clark and Jimmy Frise. It was sad to quit newspaper work. Working under Hindmarsh was like being in the German army with a poor commander."[6] After Cranston's death, Hemingway mourned his friend in a 1952 letter to Charles Fenton. "He was as badly treated by the *Toronto Star* as a man could be and that is almost as far as a man can get in being badly treated."[7]

In the late 1930s, *Toronto Star* reporters who were attempting to organize a newspaper guild sent a plea for a donation to their most famous alumnus. Hemingway replied in a long letter that began with the news that he was enclosing a cheque for one hundred dollars "to beat Hindmarsh." After a four-page tirade against his former antagonist, he closed by saying, "On second thought, I'm making it $200. I welcome the opportunity to take a swing at . . . Hindmarsh."[8]

Harry Hindmarsh became president of the *Toronto Star* after the death of his father-in-law, *Star* publisher Joseph Atkinson, in 1948. On December 19, 1956, a few weeks short of his seventieth birthday and mandatory retirement, he presented the *Star* board of directors with a letter from his family doctor, assuring them that he was in perfect health. Hindmarsh asked if his retirement could be postponed, and the board granted his request. The next day, while working in his office, he suffered a massive heart attack. In true Hindmarsh style, he died in harness.

Shortly before he died, Hindmarsh admitted that his treatment of Hemingway had been wrong, though he still insisted that Hemingway had been "temperamentally unable to conform to the routine of newspaper work or to accept direction" — the prima donna to the end. "However," he said, "I should have made some effort to persuade him to stay. I made a mistake in the way I dealt with him."[9]

Morley Callaghan went to Paris in 1928. Hemingway, by then a famous author, introduced Callaghan to his new circle of literary companions, including F. Scott Fitzgerald. Callaghan and Hemingway became lifelong friends, although the relationship was strained in Paris in June of 1929 when Callaghan knocked Hemingway down during a boxing match (after a rather drunken Fitzgerald, who was acting as timekeeper, accidentally let the round run a minute too long). Word of Hemingway being "knocked cold" by Callaghan later appeared in a New York gossip column. Hemingway wrote Callaghan three letters concerning

In January 1965, William McGeary gathered together Hemingway's surviving Toronto friends for a group interview at the Lord Simcoe Hotel to aid Carlos Baker's Hemingway biography. From left to right, they are McGeary, Roy Greenaway, Morley Callaghan, Mary Lowrey, Ernest Smith, Jimmy Cowan and Greg Clark. (Toronto Star Library)

the reports of their now infamous boxing match. These Hemingway letters — offered for sale in 1994 by Callaghan's son Barry — were stolen by thieves who cracked the safe in a Toronto antiquarian bookstore. They have not been recovered.

Callaghan, who went on to become one of Canada's most widely known authors, recalled his relationship with Hemingway in the memoir *That Summer in Paris*. He died in 1990, aged eighty-six.

Ernest Hemingway came to Toronto an unpublished writer. But by the time his years as a reporter and foreign correspondent for the *Toronto Star* had ended, he had developed into a fiction writer with a unique style. His life work — including *For Whom the Bell Tolls, A Farewell to Arms* and *The Old Man and the Sea* — earned him the Nobel Prize for literature in 1954. He is regarded by many as one of the most important fiction writers of the twentieth century.

On July 2, 1961, in his Ketchum, Idaho, home, Ernest Hemingway committed suicide by shooting himself. He was sixty-one and had been increasingly plagued by ill health and mental problems and was finding it impossible to do the things he lived for: to enjoy himself and, most important, to write.

Ernest Hemingway in Paris, 1924.
(John F. Kennedy Library)

In September of 1924, after a newspaper wire story reported that Hemingway and a friend had been gored by bulls, Hemingway wrote Greg Clark a letter from Paris, telling of his adventure the previous summer, a trip to the Feria de San Fermin in Pamplona, which would become the basis for *The Sun Also Rises*. The *Star Weekly* published it as an article on September 13, 1924. It is reprinted here for the first time in book form by way of leaving the last word to Hemingway himself.

Tackling a Spanish Bull Is "Just Like Rugby" Hemingway Tells How He Surprised the Natives

"JUST LIKE RUGBY!" WRITES ERNEST HEMINGWAY, IN A REAS-SURING letter to his friends on the *Star Weekly*, with regard to the report cabled to the newspapers in America that he, along with some adventurous friends, had been gored in the bull ring at Pamplona, Spain.

Hemingway, who was on the *Star Weekly* staff last winter, and who has been correspondent to the *Star* on several features of importance in Europe, returned to Paris from Toronto in January last.

How Hemingway got into the bull ring is due to his adventurous spirit which seeks a kick in everything from fly fishing for trout in the Pyrenees to following the Turkish army in Macedonia. His bull fighting adventures are no more startling than his turning, when he was rejected because of eye-sight by his own army during the late war, to driving a Ford truck ambulance in the Italian army, from which vantage point he managed to secure a commission in the Italian Arditi, their famous shock troops corps, in which he won the Valore medal and a lame leg.

In Paris, where he has lived for four years, except for a brief return to the *Star* last winter, he is engaged in literary work, having published two books of prose and verse, doing newspaper correspondence between times and attending prize fights, bull fights and going fishing during the respective seasons of these three major sports.

In the party with which he went down into Spain for this summer's bull fighting were John Dos Passos, author of "Three Soldiers" and other works; Donald Ogden Stewart, who writes for *Vanity Fair*; Robert McAlmon, author of "Post-Adolescence" and "A Companion Volume"; William Bird, publisher to the younger set of Paris; Mrs. Hemingway and Mrs. Bird.

In a feature article in the *Star Weekly* a year ago, Hemingway described bull fighting as it really is, an epic encounter between the brute fury of the bull and the graceful, fatal, sophistication of man. The bull fighter is an actor, not a slaughterer, an epic, heroic man, who stands out all alone in the arena, and with infinite grace and ease meets the savage onslaughts of the bull, finally, without ever descending from his pose of easy perfection, despatching the bull with a sword.

The morning of the first day of the "fiesta" of bull fighting in the town of Pamplona is a general holiday, and people are gathered from all over the country to see the ceremonies. The morning is given over to a sort of free-for-all bull fight, the arena being jammed with thousands of spectators, and anybody who likes, all the amateur bull fighters of the district, can get into the ring and face bulls which are released in the ring with horns padded.

This is the great comic relief of preceding the tragic and stately ceremony of the afternoon. It is the bulls' morning. They romp and run about the ring, where a couple of hundred excited amateurs scamper in all directions. Accidents happen. Ribs are smashed. Sometimes somebody is badly, even fatally, injured by the bulls. But for the most part it makes an uproariously funny prelude to the great performance, as the amateurs make their comic efforts to perform the graceful and formal revolutions of the real bull fighters, coming to grief on the blunt-padded horns of an infuriated and excited bull.

It was into the morning show that Hemingway and his friends entered.

Hemingway was armed with a red cape, such as the matadors use. He is a big fellow, very swift on his pins, despite the war-marked knee. He got out into the crowd, and with his red cape waved until he caught the bull's eye. And the bull, champing and stamping, prepared to charge.

Hemingway, standing sideways, and on his toes, in the approved fashion, held forth the cape and called the bull: "Toro! Toro!"

And the bull lowered his head and charged.

Instead of waving the great beast airily past him, in vain rage at the flying cape, something went wrong, and the bull struck, not the waved cape, but Hemingway, fair and square. He was what is called "coquidad."

Of course, every eye of the crowd of 18,000 souls, including his wife's, were on him, as the bull's victim. The sad finish of the excellently begun performance was succeeded by Hemingway getting one arm over the bull's horn and hanging on. Not knowing what else to do under the circumstances — this being so different from what he had seen in the bull ring, Hemingway just held on, for about ten minutes, when down went the bull in a great cloud of dust, with Hemingway on top. Algobeno and Maera, two of the great matadors of Spain, and personal friends of Hemingway, were in the ring with the rest of the crowd, just to prevent accidents, and Algobeno ran in and took hold of the bull's tail and twisted it. Between the two they threw the bull.

The whole performance so delighted the vast crowd, which had been roaring and cheering the scene meanwhile, that when Hemmy rose triumphant after the throwing, the crowd picked him up and carried him in triumph around the ring, amid shouts of acclaim.

"I was coquidad three times, Don Stewart twice," writes Hemingway. "It was just like rugby."

Previously Unrecognized Hemingway Stories

A total of thirty Hemingway stories were discovered by the author. However, for the purposes of length and other considerations, the following stories have not been reprinted here: three additional Red Ryan stories published in the *Star*, "Convicts Set Fire to Stable at 'Pen' and Made Escape," September 11, 1923, "Provincial Police Are Taking Up Chase," September 12, 1923, and "Guards Were Hoaxed by Call For Help," September 13, 1923; "Who Is He?" an unpublished *Star Weekly* feature on a certain Major Swaddling; and a long, unpublished feature on the British Coal Company (discussed on page 168). All were found in the Hemingway Collection at the John F. Kennedy Library, Boston.

Mayor Tommy Church

Tommy Church was one of Toronto's most famous political figures in the 1920s. He was elected mayor a record seven times. He never failed to see the boys off to the front in World War I and he never failed to meet a train bringing them back. But Hemingway took an instant dislike to Mayor Church, believing that he had failed to do his duty in the war. This piece — which would have been his very first Toronto Star *story — was written in January 1920, shortly after Hemingway first arrived in Toronto. But the attack on Mayor Church was a little too heavy-handed for* Star Weekly *editors, who rejected the piece. Afterwards, a disgusted Hemingway tossed the manuscript to Dorothy Connable, who saved it and later gave a copy of it to the* Star's *librarian, William McGeary.*

Mind you, I do not call Mayor Tommy Church
a slacker. He may have had many airtight exemp-
tions, certainly physical defects would prevent a
man from being accepted. They could usually be
waived if the man really wanted to join up with
something. But that is not the point.

From the standpoint of an interested observer,
why should an unmarried man of Mayor Church's
age, no matter how well exempted, who took no
active part in the war, be so popular with the returned men?

Church is undeniably popular with the returned
men. Is it because of his military record? You will
see a great many men on the streets of Toronto
wearing returned buttons who are older than
Church. Many of them had wives and families. It
was not a young man's war.

I remember in an old school house on the lower
Piave River seeing a white haired man seated
against the wall looking glumly at the blood-soaked
emergency dressing that covered the shattered
stump at his wrist.

While we were waiting our turn on the table I
spoke to him. He was a volunteer. His home was
in Abruzzi. He would be fifty-five years old next
month. He grunted his answers and looked at the
wall.

"You're too old, Dad, for this war," I said. He
resented that. The glum look left his face. He

sneered. That sneer included me, my youth, all illusions and war itself.

"Corpo di Bacco!" he snapped. "I can die as well as any man."

Sometimes when I hear how popular Mayor Church is with the returned men, I think of that old man in the cellar of the school house at Fornaci in his dirty gray green uniform looking glumly at where his hand had been.

But Church gave the troops a splendid welcome when they came home. He worked day and night making speeches. He thanked them all. He kept the home fires burning while they were away.

And he gets away with it.

New Ether to Credit of Toronto Surgeon

This unsigned news story, published in the Star *January 27, 1920, is one of five stories identified as the work of Hemingway by the late* Star *librarian William McGeary (see page 62 for full story). It was Hemingway's first* Star *article, appearing three weeks before "Circulating Pictures a New High-Art Idea in Toronto," his first previously identified article. Memoirs by Hemingway's sister and brother both verify that he wrote home to say his first* Star *story was to interview a "medical man."*

The new ether, perfected by Dr. James H. Cotton, a young Toronto surgeon residing at 24 Bloor Street East, has been proclaimed in the papers of the United States as one of the most important discoveries in medical science for many years. Once again, it would seem, the prophet has not been appreciated or encouraged in his own country. As far back as May, 1916, Dr. C.K. Clarke, the present dean at the University, wrote to the press in enthusiastic terms about the new discovery, but nothing was done. Today Toronto hospitals are buying the "Cotton Process Ether" from the great DuPont firm, which has perfected the manufacture of the product at last.

New ether's action

There are many things claimed for the new ether, which is really a development of the old that was discovered in Boston many years ago. It acts more quickly, almost eliminates the nausea that follows the use of ordinary ether, allows many operations, even of a major character, such as the removal of an appendix, or a deep-seated growth, to be accomplished without the patient losing consciousness, and gives up its hold on the patient inhaling it almost as soon as the cone or tube is removed from the face or nostrils. Compared to the old ethers and anesthetics, only about one-quarter of the quantity needs to be used and sleep can always be induced by the addition of a few drops more.

"In the ether that I have perfected," Dr. Cotton once explained, "there is no reaction, because sensation is blocked. With the old ether, you could have the patient drunk, and yet the sensory nerves would not be blocked. With the new ether the mind can be made a complete blank."

Idea came in 1915

The idea came to Dr. Cotton in 1915, the year he graduated in medicine. He had been interested in chemistry even when he was attending Harbord Collegiate and followed his bent in a course of Physiology and Biochemistry, which led to a B.A. degree, then an M.A. degree, at Toronto University, before he entered medicine.

The first promising results took place when a number of animals were able to be relieved from pain without going to sleep. At this time, May, 1916, the material could only be manufactured very slowly, one pound every three weeks, and it cost $80 a pound. It was offered as a discovery to the Toronto General Hospital, and the University of Toronto, combined, to do what they willed with it for war purposes.

Eight months to prepare

In June, 1917, a paper and demonstration were given at the Royal Victoria Hospital, Montreal, with two operations. The result was so satisfactory that the new product received the active approbation of the whole Dominion Association. The Du-Pont people, who approached Dr. Cotton then, only received the complete rights of the new discovery, after the delay in Toronto, and then to speed up processes and production for war purposes. It took exactly 8 months to produce in quantity even then, after the intricate secret process had been handed over.

Another important aspect of the discovery is in its relation to crime.

"It is capable," said Dr. Cotton, "of making the most hardened criminal tell the truth, and nothing but the truth."

Truth-telling Ether a Secret

This story, a February 7, 1920 follow-up to the "New Ether" story that appeared on January 27, has been identified as Hemingway's work by William McGeary (see page 62).

Unfortunately for jealous wives, detectives and truth seekers in general, Dr. James H. Cotton's new ether, as produced commercially for the surgical and dental professions, does not make the patient tell the truth, the whole truth and nothing but the truth.

During Dr. Cotton's research work, an ether combination was discovered which did that very thing. And Dr Cotton could supply governments, if it were considered in the interests of humanity, with that secret formula. No doubt, private enterprises will immediately set to work experimenting on that other miraculous ether, and we will see cunning advertisements of "Veracity Ether, recommended to suspicious wives, detectives, politicians, etc." For during these experiments in 1916 and 1917, Dr Cotton was constrained to stop some of his subjects from telling the unvarnished stories of their lives.

The perfected "Cotton process ether" now being used in great quantities in Toronto hospitals was designed for the purposes of surgery alone. After four years of uphill fighting on the part of Dr. Cotton and the group of physicians and surgeons who supported and encouraged him, his discovery is being manufactured by one of the greatest corporations in the world (the duPont de Nemours Company) and is being accepted in Dr. Cotton's native city as a revolutionizing contribution to medical science.

The romance surrounding the production of the new anesthetic, while not appealing to Dr. Cotton as a research man, is full of that quality which makes the scientist's labors appeal to the layman.

Dr. Cotton, who is the son of the late Dr. John H. Cotton, is not yet thirty years of age. At Varsity he took, in addition to the combined Arts and Medical courses, the Physics course which is in a separate faculty entirely. In 1915, after graduation, while serving the prescribed period in Toronto General Hospital, Dr. Cotton was brought in close contact with the anesthetic work of surgery. And this contact convinced him that there was wide scope for improvement in the physical qualities of the anesthetics used. He therefore embarked on research and devoted himself intensely to the study of ether, and its possibilities.

May replace all others
In 1916, Dr. Cotton had made appreciable progress, and a demonstration was given, as a result of which one of this city's greatest physicians made a public statement in recognition of a great advance having been made in the subject of anesthetics. Nothing came of this, however, no professional acceptance was made of the new ether.

Dr. Cotton thereupon completed his research, bringing forth an ether which, if administered in small quantities, induced what is called analgesia, or loss of sensation, but not putting the patient to sleep, and if administered in greater quantities, put the patient sound asleep. Here, then, was an ether that could be easily applied either for minor things such as dental work or dressings, when it was not necessary for the patient to be asleep, or for major operations, when the patient could be asleep.

Its greatest advantage over former anesthetics is that on an average only two ounces of it are required against an average ten ounces of the old, that it works much more quickly, and that it causes no nausea or sickness, after the operation. These counts make it look as if operations would be a pleasure.

Having completed his work and having appeared before a congress of the Dominion Medical Association in Montreal, early in 1917, with a complete account of his work, Dr. Cotton was approached by representatives of the duPont Company.

Dr. Cotton, however, wrote instead to the Toronto General Hospital and the University of Toronto, offering his discovery to them, to be used by them for manufacture, sale or royalties or however they saw fit.

No replies were received. Dr. Cotton waited eight months for replies to his letters, and then, in order to give his discovery to the world and especially to the soldiers overseas, the war being then at its height, accepted the offer of the duPont Company.

Dr. Cotton then made every effort to be sent overseas as a medical officer, in spite of the fact that he was seriously disqualified physically, feeling he had material that would be of real value to the military medical problems. He was, however, unable to secure a post.

He further developed various appliances for the administration of the new ether. There is only one operation in which the Cotton process ether cannot be used, and that is in the case of tonsils, and this lone exception is true only when a wrong method of applying that ether is used. By means of the "semi-closed" method, operations on tonsils are absolutely as successful as any other.

In teeth extraction, etc., the patient, while awake, is not conscious of any pain.

This ether is now being used by practically all Toronto hospitals, is being manufactured and used in tremendous quantities in the United States, and Dr. George Carveth, chief anaesthetist at the Western Hospital, states that it soon will be used to the exclusion of all other ethers throughout the profession.

Red Flag in Toronto

As discussed on page 66, there is strong evidence to suggest that this humorous feature, which appeared February 14, 1920, was one of Hemingway's first Star Weekly *articles. As William McGeary points out, the phraseology and subject matter suggest the author was newly arrived from Chicago, as was Hemingway at the time this appeared.*

Sam Stoichi arrived in Toronto by freight, let go his armful of rods in the freight yards east of Bathurst Street, dusted the cinders off, and walked up-town.

Sam was a Red, not of any philosophical reason, but because he was from Slacho-Bulramia; and all his friends and relations were Red. But when the big raid came in the United States, and many of Sam's noisier compatriots were snatched off to far prisons, Sam made a frantic dash for the border, and "grabbing an armful of rods," as the hoboes say came by stealth into Canada.

A rather dazed and weary Sam walked up Bathurst Street to Queen. He had a few Yankee coins in his pocket. For, while being a Red was a pleasant and thrilling occupation, it was not lucrative, yet.

Sam turned east on Queen, dropped into a Greek restaurant and had sausages and mashed potatoes to recuperate his energy.

Refreshed, he sallied forth into the street, with a keen eye peeled for fellow countrymen. Queen Street is cosmopolitan. He saw no end of people who looked like Slacho-Bulramians, but he hadn't the luck to strike one who answered his subdued greeting in his native tongue.

Suddenly Sam's quick eye saw something that froze him in his tracks.

His mouth fell open. His eyes popped. And a deep gasp rose from his diaphragm.

There, suspended lazily in the crisp winter air from the doorway of a shop was the Red flag!

Sam blinked. He moved aside to get a better focus. Yes! Sure enough, it was the Red flag. And by all that was holy to a Bolshevik, there was a meeting going on in the shop.

Sam had only seen the Red flag in the secrecy of the dimmest and deepest cellars in Chicago, where only the boldest of the Reds were assembled. But there, on Queen Street in broad daylight, the

Red flag waved and the crowds rolled by unconcerned.

Sam, fearing he had suffered a mental lapse, crept warily closer to the shop. After half a dozen long pauses, and agonized scrutinies, Sam got near enough to hear someone making a most spirited speech within the shop of the Red flag.

Then Sam had one more violent shock. He beheld a gigantic policeman, blowing on his cold hands, standing in the entrance of the meeting place. But the policeman had a serene and jovial expression on his face.

That decided it. Canada had had the revolution, and Sam hadn't heard of it while in hiding! That was it. The Red flag had come, and the workers were supreme!

Sam straightened his back, twisted up his sandy moustache and boldly walked in among the comrades.

The meeting was crowded. Sam was a little disappointed to see so many women present. But he glued his eyes on the speaker, who stood on a little platform.

The speaker was making a very Red speech by the sound of it, although Sam couldn't understand English. The speaker, thought Sam, didn't look unlike Comrade Trotsky.

"How much am I offered, ladies and gents?" shouted the speaker. "This beautiful baby carriage,

solid vicker mit gold finishings on it! How much!
How much!"

"Swadoba! Zrashto! Neuski Prospekt!" cried
Sam, from the back of the crowd, his voice boom-
ing with enthusiasm.

The speaker looked a little rattled, then went on,
"Come now, ladies, one of you needs dis lovely big
baby carriage, ain't it? How much!"

"Trotsky! Omsk! Dvina!" roared Sam, thrilled
with the spirit, if not with the letter, of the speaker's
words.

The crowd turned curious eyes on Sam. The
speaker leaned over his raised platform, aimed a
little hammer at Sam and yelled, "Say, Mister,
what is it you got! A bad cold?"

Sam, somewhat disgusted at the tameness of the
meeting, but filled with the ardour of the Cause,
smiled back.

"Come now!" shouted the speaker more earnestly
after the interruption, "Ain't anybody got a kid
for dis wonderful, gold-finished, solid vicker baby
carriage, dat is come out of one of our best Rose-
dale homes?"

"Lenine! Dobrudja!" yelled Sam, applaudingly.

"Hey!" cried the speaker, turning suddenly and
impatiently. "Mister policeman!"

The policeman moved in from the doorway.

"Run dat fresh guy in! He's trying to put dis
sale on de bum!"

The policeman singled out Sam.

"Come on, here," said the policeman. "On your way! Beat it!"

And Sam found himself rudely pushed out of the meeting.

He struggled, twisted, and in vain tried to explain in his own language that he was a Comrade, a Red of the Reds, a fellow agitator, fleeing from persecution.

He merely made the policeman mad. He was held firmly at a telegraph post till a terrible black wagon called for him and his guard.

At the police station, the constable said, "This fresh bohunk tried to bust up an auction sale."

The Superman Myth

Although bylined, this "Superman Myth" boxing article was overlooked when the supposedly comprehensive works were assembled in Dateline, Toronto, *perhaps because it appeared in an unusual place — the* Star *editorial page of June 25, 1921. In it, Hemingway predicts Jack Dempsey will lose his upcoming championship bout with French boxer Georges Carpentier. Hemingway was so sure of the outcome that he bet $50 on Carpentier. (Dempsey won by a knockout in the fourth round.)*

BY ERNEST M. HEMINGWAY

Jack Dempsey, a well-built, scowling, hard faced citizen of Utah, is regarded as a superman by several millions of people.

He has been pronounced the greatest fighter of all time, the hardest hitter, and the fastest heavyweight that ever climbed through the ropes. Many people fear for the safety of Georges Carpentier's life, when he shuts himself into the ring with this tremendous primitive force.

Most persons acquainted with things pugilistic believe that Jack Dempsey won the title of heavyweight champion of the world from Jess Willard at Toledo, Ohio, July 4th, 1919. The formal transfer of the crown did take place there — but Jess Willard lost the title in the Baltimore Hotel in Kansas City, Missouri.

Willard's stupid, kindly face, flushed by his efforts to make the best of the last few months before the strict enforcement of the 18th amendment, was one of the landmarks of the Baltimore. Jess Willard hated fighting and he was very fond of drinking. That doesn't make an ideal temperament for a fighter — but Willard never was a fighter at heart.

Picked by fate and Jack Curley, to be the man to defeat the renegade Johnson in a bout that had been in bad odor with every one acquainted with the back-stage workings of championship fighters, Willard became the champion. He defended his title once in a no decision fight against Frank Moran, a mediocre opponent, and then lapsed into more congenial pursuits.

On July 4th, 40 years old, heavy, paunched, untrained and sodden and loggy with two years of steady drinking, he went forth with cow-like courage to fight Jack Dempsey for the championship of the world and $150,000 win, lose or draw. In the first round the slim, sun-browned Dempsey slugged him to the canvas seven times. Willard looked dumbly and stupidly up at the tiger-like youth and staggered to his feet to earn his $150,000. At the end of the third round Dempsey was tired from smashing the big bulk and Willard seemed to be recuperating from the beating he had taken. Willard seemed the fresher of the two — Dempsey was hanging on to him and occasionally socking in a tired manner.

Willard's seconds tossed in a towel at the start of the fourth round. Jess believed he had given the fans a run for their admission — and he didn't need the championship any more — he had $150,000.

That is the way Dempsey won the championship of the world. Since then he has fought twice. The first fight was with Billy Miske, a St. Paul light-heavyweight, and a close personal friend of Dempsey. Miske had been under a doctor's care for over a year and was unable to earn a living in the ring due to physical disability.

Dempsey gave Miske a crack at the "title" and incidentally a guarantee of $25,000 for his services. Miske, looking the sick man he was, made a few feeble leads at Dempsey. Dempsey hippodromed for a while and then abandoned friendship and speedily slugged Miske into unconsciousness — and the possession of $25,000.

Experts all over the country hailed the victory as a Dempsey superman triumph and only a few came out with the statement of Miske's true condition. In February the boxing fans refused to become wrought up over Dempsey's coming fight with Big Bill Brennan. It looked like another set-up. A few wagers were laid as to what round Dempsey would knock out the second-rate Chicago heavyweight.

Between the Miske and Brennan fights, however, Dempsey had been doing his training on Broadway, and his road work, some said, along the gay white way that has stopped more fighters than all the left hooks and right crosses in the world.

Dempsey entered the ring, the night of the Brennan fight, trembling like a scared school girl. His nerves were gone and his face, according to ringsiders, was a ghastly green color. No one could have recognized him as the brown-skinned, finely trained, young slugger who had cut down the ponderous Willard.

For twelve rounds Dempsey had all he could do to stay in the ring with the cumbersome, slow-moving, but awkwardly hard-hitting Brennan. In the twelfth round he knocked Brennan out with "the rabbit punch," a blow that is barred as a foul everywhere but in the United States.

Nearly every fight writer present said that if anyone but Brennan had been fighting Dempsey, the title would have changed hands. The superman myth seemed to be exploded. But now it is back again in full force.

"Throw out the Brennan fight," says Jack Kearns, Dempsey's manager, "don't pay any attention to it. It doesn't mean anything."

But why should it be "thrown out"? What has Dempsey done since that shows he is any more of a fighter than when he fought Brennan?

Jack Dempsey is not the man today that he was at Toledo. Two years of championship life coupled with whatever effects there might be from his wild years as a bum and tramp fighter have made a change in him. The public are rarely told of these things.

Before the Jeffries-Johnson fight, everyone in Jeffries' camp knew that it was a crime to allow him to enter the squared circles against the negro fighter. Jeffries was a wreck from high living. But who announced it before the fight?

Jim Corbett, who trained Jeffries, said the day before the bout: "It is an outrage to allow him to face Johnson." But what papers published the statement till after the battle?

Georges Carpentier has a chance on July 2nd that is the envy of half a dozen fighters.

Harry Greb, who knocked out Soldier Jones in Toronto early this spring, said the other day: "The Frenchman is lucky — any good fast man, who can hit, will take Jack Dempsey. I envy Carpentier his chance."

That is an inside opinion on the big fight.

What Professional Boxers Fight For

This stream-of-consciousness boxing typescript was mailed by Hemingway to Greg Clark from Chicago in June of 1921, along with the "Superman Myth" story. But it was rejected by Star *sports editor Bill Hewitt, according to a letter Clark wrote to Hemingway. The typescript was found in the Hemingway Collection.*

What professional boxers fight for is for money. No amateur boxers stay in amateur boxing many years if they are hit much. The amateurs who stay in as amateurs a long time are those who are hard to hit and who know how to administer lots of punishment. They like it. If they turned professionals they would be hit plenty and they would not like it.

Now Mr. Lardner and Mr. Pegler are both pros. They write for money. Or rather Mr. Lardner did and Mr. Pegler does. But they are intellectuals. Otherwise why would they feel superior to another pro who, taking a left hook that he did not see as the right missed, they slugging, not because they like to but because if you don't fight instead of box you can't make a living, going down with a foolish expression, shaking his head, come on and fight, getting up, go on finish the bastard, seeing the next one all right, but his arms weigh a ton apiece and he can't get them up to block it.

Come on, kill the spick of spicks, get him Tony, in the belly, in the belly, bring his hands down, now you got him, oh baby, did you see that one, get up you yellow bastard, watch yourself Tony, watch yourself boy, oh *baby* did you see that one, then after that one his jaw felt like a bag of marbles but it was all like a slow motion picture now and at the bell he walked to Tony's corner and they went over and grabbed him. It certainly is an amusing sport, the cauliflower industry, where nothing's comic-er than walking on the heels; somebody elses heels.

They'll write and cry about each other. So noble, so good to his folks, against suggestive songs, no dirty words. But they're superior to those who make it with their hands, the nightly tragic somewhere of their combat, a body punch hurts just as hard in Keokuk, nobody ever liked them there,

and the language that they speak they will distort
into a very comic diction, so that you'll never hear
the resin squeak, nor see the cords flex, leaning
on them before coming out, and so we have, from
them, the Orchid Man, and never Carp untrained,
the fight supposed to be fixed, double crossed by
Siki after he hit him too hard in the third, coming
up off the floor, to take for four rounds the worst
beating a white man ever took from black while
Descamps ran into the jig's corner between every
round begging him to quit, with Siki leaning back
and shaking those big, bleeding lips; and from them
do we get Harry Greb's nose like a sunken trowell,
and him going around Convention Hall that time
before he fought Soldier Jones wearing a cap and
wanting to know if anyone wanted to bet on the
fight. It was his first time in Toronto. And nobody
did. Then him finally getting a bet Greb would
knock him out in the fourth. Giving four to one
he could name the round. And in the first Jones
coming out and saying, "All right you German son
of a bitch," and Greb dropping him before he
thought and having to hold him up and promise
Lou Marsh, who wanted to throw them out of the
ring that there was going to be action during the
next three rounds and there wasn't. To come out
in the fourth and feint once and let the right go
and turn and walk back to his corner without even
looking around while Lou counted. Or one time
seeing Bobby Ebor duck a right swing and catch

it on the ear and that organ come up before our eyes first·like a plum, then like a bunch of grapes and finally it was a purple organ. (This would be a scream to them. The sowing of the cauliflower.) This other guy couldn't hit it again so it didn't burst and Bobby came in all out of focus to his corner and the bird who was handling him bit a little piece out and sucked it neatly down, spitting it into the water bucket. Somebody hollered to the referee who was watching, "Hey. What's that guy do in civil life?" (Toronto's full of wits) and the referee, the side of his hand to his lips, "He's either a what-do-you-call-it or a barber and the son-of-a-such claims he's never shaved a man in his life."

See how clean we keep it?

Genoa Scrubs Up for Peace Parley

Hemingway covered the Genoa Conference in April of 1922, sending back a flurry of dispatches including this article, which appeared under Hemingway's byline on April 15, 1922. It does not appear in the Dateline, Toronto *collection.*

BY ERNEST M. HEMINGWAY

Special Correspondence of the *Star*

GENOA, April 15. – In spite of being the most disillusioned nation at the peace conference, the Italians take the Genoa Conference with terrific seriousness and enthusiasm.

Genoa is scrubbed cleaner than it ever was before or ever will be again. Orders were issued, after a press correspondent had commented on it humorously, against the fine Italian custom of hanging all the washing out of the window, and after the first few days the night clothes of Genoa no longer flapped beside the Union Jack and the Tricolor. Narrow streets are scrubbed clean, buildings painted, everything in Genoa smells of varnish, from the Royal Palace to the co-operative wine shops.

Rosy faced boy soldiers in the smart grey-green uniform of the Royal Guards are stationed before every building, and at each side of all streets, alleys and courts. The kid soldiers look embarrassed and exalted by the automatic pistols and workmanlike bayonets that hang from their belts, and smile shyly and answer in the soft, Roman dialect when I ask them directions.

"We are new soldiers, signor, we have never been in Genoa before, and we know only the place where the corporal puts us."

The old Roman quarter of Genoa has the narrowest streets in the world. Most of them are not wide enough for good sized sidewalks, and the buildings rise five stories high, bulging out and nearly meeting at the top. Down these stone slab-paved streets, at all hours of the day and night, comes running the ambulance; mounted on rubber tires it is tipped like an operating table, covered with a white shroud and pulled by six men who run alongside like the jinrick-shaw pullers in Japan hustling it through streets where a horse or motor ambulance could never penetrate.

Newspaper correspondents from all over the

world are housed in an Albergo dei Giornaliste or
Hotel for Journalists, on the top of a high hill overlooking the harbor. Busses leave the hotel for the
press headquarters every fifteen minutes, taking
twenty minutes to make a journey that is not more
than half a mile as the crow flies. The hills of
Genoa are so steep and the road so tortuous and
congested that any sort of travel on wheels is very
unpleasant. The cobbles jolt, the busses lurch, the
people in the streets point at the bus with its official
coat of arms, and wonder which of the forty some
nations at the conference are riding in it.

Press headquarters is in a palace in the heart
of the city, and is full of a throng of men all speaking different languages, and all pounding ridicu-
lously small typewriters with a look of concentra-
tion on their faces, or else writing in illegible
longhand at the twenty tables scattered over the
room. An elaborate bar has been fitted up with
rows of bottles of Scotch, Irish and American rye
whiskey, but it is deserted except for an occasional
journalist who rushes in and demands a glass of
milk and a sandwich. Genoa is not a drinking conference. There is too much work to do, the delegations are scattered fifteen and twenty miles apart
along the coast, and the newspapermen work like
street laborers twelve and fifteen hours a day.

Just when a few tired journalists will be getting
out of the bus at the Albergo del Giornaliste to
take a much needed bath and get the dust of the

long ride to Rapallo out of their hair and eyes, someone will bring word that, "the British are receiving at the Miramare." It is a long ride back all the way across Genoa and up the hills on the other side to the great Miramare Hotel, where all the correspondents will be crowded into a room and around a long table, while Sir Edward Grigg, Lloyd George's secretary, tells them in matter of fact tones what has happened that day in council meeting.

"Can you get us a copy of Lloyd George's speech that he is to deliver?" someone asked from around the table.

"He doesn't know what he is going to say himself," Sir Edward answers. "All day he has been going around saying, 'What shall I say there tomorrow?' You know he never speaks except with the most fragmentary notes."

"No, there will be no supreme council," Sir Edward says. "This whole conference is designed to get away from the idea of the conquered and the conqueror, and so all nations are to meet on an equal footing. Anything else, gentlemen?"

If there is not, the newspapermen go out, "Good night, Sir Edward."

The newspaper correspondents walk down the hill in little bunches to where they can get cabs to the telegraph office. If nothing else happens the day is over.

Interpreters Make or Mar Speeches at Genoa Parley

Hemingway greatly exaggerates his grasp of foreign languages in this overlooked and uncollected article that was sent from the Genoa Conference. It appeared under Hemingway's byline in the Star *of April 15, 1922.*

BY ERNEST M. HEMINGWAY

Special Correspondence of the *Star*

GENOA — Interpreters can make or break any speech and they break some three thousand per cent more speeches than they ever make.

All of the public proceedings of the Genoa conference were translated into three languages. Barthou, heading the French delegation, had the best interpreter; a man who translates instantly from French into English in a clear, ringing voice losing not one single inflection of the original speech.

Consequently, Barthou's speeches were correctly and fully reported in the press of the world. Because they were improved on, if anything, in translation.

Chancellor Wirth, of Germany, lost almost the entire effectiveness of his very able speech at the opening of the conference because the interpreter garbled the words in such a manner that they were absolutely impossible to understand in either French or English. Only those who understood German in the hall knew what Wirth had said until the day after his speeches when they appeared in the verbatim report of conference proceedings.

Wirth's interpreter was a wild-haired, wild-eyed young man, who, someone whispered in the press gallery while he was talking, was born in Chicago and spoke 22 languages. I believe he speaks them all equally badly. His excitement was so great at his exalted position that his voice shook and trembled and the words were lost in the flow of heavily mouthed accents. Consequently hardly a word of Wirth's speech appeared in the papers next day. The reporters had not understood it.

Tchitcherin, head of the Russian delegation, speaks both French and English, and he too is almost impossible to understand, because of his defect in speech of which I have spoken. His voice is the most peculiar I have ever heard, the s's being hissed beyond all belief and a queer, metallic, like sandpaper, running through all the diction. His French is easier to understand than his English.

No one realizes his own limitations in speaking better than Tchitcherin and when he had some rapid fire controversy on, he always spoke in French, leaving the translation to M. Barthou's interpreter with the wonderful clear voice. In this way Tchitcherin was sure that he would secure correct reporting of his speech.

Before You Go on a Canoe Trip, Learn Canoeing

This outdoor feature, which in many ways suggests the style of Hemingway short stories such as "Big Two-Hearted River," was identified as his work by both William McGeary and Greg Clark (see page 81 for more discussion). It was published without a byline in the Toronto Star *on June 3, 1922.*

"We are going on a canoe trip up to Algonquin Park," writes a lady to the editor, "two girls and our husbands. As we have never been in a canoe and have only been motor picnicking, what advice can you give us for our trip?"

The first thing a beginner at canoe cruising should do is to spend as many afternoons as possible between now and the time of his departure, on the Humber, learning what a frail, tippy, treacherous and altogether delightful craft a canoe is.

He should learn to handle his canoe in wind and wave, and should practice paddling it loaded with three people in it, as a loaded canoe is even trickier than a lighter one.

If your experience of outings has been restricted to picnics by motor car, then you are in very grave danger as a canoeist. For the first and last thing about canoe cruising and camping is the necessity of reducing baggage to the absolute minimum.

Put it this way: as nearly all canoe trips involve portages, you must get all your belongings into as few packages as possible, and yet you must be able to carry those packages comfortably for distances ranging from 500 yards to two miles.

The ideal cruiser, the half-breed guide of the north bush, makes a portage in one trip. He carries his canoe on his head, and all his belongings in a pack on his back.

There's your standard. You will in most cases have to make two trips to a portage, the first time over with your canoe, and the second trip over with your dunnage. If that dunnage is in a score of separate pieces, instead of being packed neatly and economically in a dunnage bag, you are going to have your trip ruined. I have seen many a haggard and fed-up camping party struggling over the portage trails with unmanageable dunnage. When they pull their canoe ashore, it is laden with loose gear. Pots and pans are shoved up under the decks or lying loose on the baggage. The tent, damp and therefore loosely and largely folded, is taking up half the space of the craft amidships. Poorly packed bags and heaped up, with blankets, clothing and stuff, and wooden boxes of grub are perched perilously on top of all. They dump all this junk out and carry the canoe over the trail, then come wearily back for the baggage, which is more than a load, not only because it is more kit than they should have brought on a canoe trip, but because it is poorly packed, in small pieces, instead of in one or two large pieces that can be comfortably toted on the back.

Even on a fairly long camping trip, your dunnage should be no heavier nor bulkier than you can comfortably carry on your back. You can determine this before you set out. And by dunnage is meant everything except the canoe and the paddles — tent, food, blankets, pots and pans, and personal baggage.

Put everything in bags. Take no boxes, no bottles. The brown canvas dunnage bag about three feet long and a foot in diameter, is the best size, commodious and handy. One blanket, one change of underwear, a rubber sheet, a light raincoat or slicker, should be all the clothing taken. If the weather is chilly, sleep in your raincoat and extra socks.

If two are in a canoe, one man should take the tent in his bag and the other should take the grub in his. This means cutting personal kit down to the bone. The pots and pans, of the smallest size and fewest number, should be equally divided between the two bags, and small canvas sacks should be made to put these dirty utensils in, or about the second day they will be found constituting a part of that bunch of disagreeable small junk, which usually includes axes, fishing rods, cans of food, boots and cameras, which litters the bottom of the canoe, and makes every portage a blasted nuisance.

The ideal canoe is this: there are thongs on the thwarts into which the paddles fit for portaging. The axe is hitched snugly under the floor board. Amidships, side by side, lie two dunnage bags, with their tump lines attached. One six-foot fishing rod is stowed ready for sport under the thwarts. Not another thing, unless it be the knee cushions, are loose in that canoe.

If food absolutely must be taken which won't go into the two dunnage bags, be sure that it is at least in a bag, and as small a bag as possible. For food is the heaviest thing to be taken.

A side of bacon, cakes of dried soup, butter in a tin, jam in a tin, tea and sugar in small salt bags, condensed milk if you must have milk, then cans of beans, meat, etc. A box of patent pancake flour is a good thing. Empty it into a tin. Take no glass. If you can't get bread along the line, take what you will need in a separate bag, and make it a regrettable separate bundle on the line of march.

A cotton flour bag makes a good bread bag. A general rule covering grub is to seek that which is in the smallest and most keepable form. Many foods spoil when opened.

If you are going into the far bush where bread is not within a day's paddle, better learn to make biscuits from mother, take along a small tin folding reflector oven and a bag of flour and "burn your own."

Motor campers have no conception of the need for economy in kit in canoe cruising.

The great point is — cut, cut, cut. Weed out something from your kit every time you look at it in preparation. Go easy on the clothes. You will sleep in them anyway, most likely, and you must wash linen as you go: Wash at night and dry by the camp fire.

A warning about canoes: A lot of dish-shaped pleasure canoes are being made nowadays which are murder on a canoe trip. Be sure to rent a good, wide-bellied canoe that will carry a load in wind and wave. Rented canoes are often old fellows that have been painted so often they have about 50 lbs. of white lead on them. Pick the lightest and roomiest 15 or 16-foot canoe available.

If you don't wear your old clothes from the city, be sure to leave your city duds in a hotel or with a settler at your jumping-off place.

The public library has some excellent books on cruising and camping. Go into the central branch and look up camping in the card index. The assistants will be glad to get the book for you or to notify you by post card when it is in.

Nothing but experience will teach you camping, however. The books will give you valuable hints. But there never was such a thing as a born camper.

They are made, not born.

Talking with the Tiger

In September of 1922, Hemingway interviewed former French premier Georges Clemenceau (see page 134). Although this colorful article contains dialogue that is closer to fiction than journalism in style, it was not rejected by the Star *on these grounds. Rather, managing editor John Bone felt Clemenceau's erroneous statement that all Canadians had refused compulsory service during World War I would be insulting to Canadian readers. The typescript was found in JFK Library.*

Les Sables-D'Ollone, France. — "That is the house of M. Clemenceau." The chauffeur pointed.

The car turned into a road that ran straight down to the sea and we saw a low, white cottage set on a sandy headland. There was a barbed wire fence around the stakes jutting out of the sand, and on

the sea-ward side a slim, white flagpole supported
a great, red banner that waved and flapped in the
wind.

Another car had turned into the road just ahead
of us and we followed it through the gate in the
barbed wire fence and stopped at the door of the
cottage. A man of about forty-five got out of the
car ahead of us and entered the cottage carrying
a basket of groceries. His wife, in motoring clothes,
followed him in. The Clemenceau cook in a white
apron came out and took our cards.

The man who had carried in the groceries came
out of the other end of the cottage and waved to
us.

"Will you come and wait in my father's bed-
room?" he said in French.

We walked ankle deep through the sand to the
middle of the long cottage and Clemenceau's son
waved us to enter the low doorway. "It will only
be a minute," he explained, and was gone again.

The room was of plain boards. On one side was
a wash stand with a basin and pitcher, on the other
a writing desk. In back of the sofa where I sat
was a comfortable bed. Over the bed was a book-
case. On the wall, the only ornaments were the
mounted heads of antelope and buck Clemenceau
had shot on his trip to India. Over the writing desk
was a big crocodile's head with open jaws and silly-
looking glass eyes. But the thing that caught and
held your eye was a tiger skull that was nailed up

over the window facing the sea. It was bone white
and polished and the two big teeth coming down
represented the Clemenceau mustache. It looked
exactly like the cartoons of the Old Tiger himself.
I had gotten up to look at the titles of the books
on the shelf above the writing desk and had only
noted one, "The History Of Buddhism" when we
heard voices coming from the back of the cottage.
Round the corner of the cottage, walking in the
deep sand, came Clemenceau's son and Clemenceau himself walking with the son's wife, his arm
through hers. A bulky man, thickened by age,
wearing a brown tweed suit, a funny, flat cap, his
face as brown as an Ojibway, his white mustache
drooping, his white eye-brows bushy, looking the
tiger his pictures show him, his eyes twinkling as
he talked to his plump daughter-in-law, he came
plodding through the sand. They stopped in front
of the door. "Au revoir papa!" The woman bent
toward him to kiss him. Clemenceau put his arms
around her and kissed her.

"Au revoir, my child. See you soon." They went
on to their car and he came plodding into the room.
His eyes smiled. They are the only things you can
see while you are talking to him. They seem to
get inside of your eyes somehow and fasten claws
there. When he is talking all his brown, healthy,
Chinese mandarin's face seems to have nothing to
do with them. But his eyes smiled at us.

"Good day, gentlemen," he said in English. "It is a hard place to get to, isn't it? Come, we'll go to a better place to talk."

He motioned us to go out of the door ahead of him. I hesitated. "Go on. Go on." He put his hand on my back for me to go ahead.

In a sun room built onto the other end of the cottage and furnished with four big wicker chairs he stopped.

"Here we are," he said, smiling. "Now, which is Mr. Bird and which Mr. Hemingway? Good. It is a shame you have made such a long trip. I wired you last night not to come. I have not given interviews. But now you are here we can talk." His eyes twinkled. "Sit down, gentlemen."

We sat down and I looked at him closely. His face is remarkably like a Chinaman's. If the mustache, instead of being large and drooping, was cut in a narrow line, he would look exactly like a Mandarin. He was wearing a stand-up collar and a ready-tied, black bow tie and his gray-gloved hands rested in his lap. He speaks English jerkily, fluently, colloquially and with a French accent.

"I am glad Kipling said those things," he began in his concise, jerky manner. "They are true. But they are unfair. When the *New York World* cabled me to ask a reply to Kipling's statement, I said, 'no.'" The "no" chopped off and final as it used to be in the conferences of the big four at Versailles.

"Then I went out and took a walk and thought 'yes, I will reply.'

"I have been thinking about going to the United States for the last three months and I thought, 'Here is a good chance to go and tell the Americans the truth.'" His eyes smiled.

Then I asked a question that waked the tiger in him, the tiger that always sleeps with one eye open and that when roused changes him from a very amiable and kind old gentleman to the wrecker of ministries, the man who is still the most dangerous political power in France.

"We are hoping you will come to Canada, sir," I said. At the word Canada his face went tiger. His eyes fastened into me and he leaned forward.

"I will not come to Canada." He jerked, emphasizing the not like an insult. "The Canadians rejected compulsory service and refused to help France."

"But," I said, "that was not Canada as a whole. The Canadian Army." He had not listened to anything I had said. His face was still tiger.

"I know," he said, busy with his own thoughts. "I know. It was the influence of the Catholic priests. I know."

"But how about the rest of Canada. Not French Canada. Ontario. The *Star* invites you to come to Toronto."

"No, no, no," he jerked. "I can't do it. I can't do it. I can't mix things. I go to America only on a definite mission to explain the position of France to the people of the United States. I can't mix things. It is impossible to come to Toronto." He shook his head.

"Will you send a message to Canada?" I asked. "What you have said about military service will not be very palatable. Besides it is not just to the rest of Canada."

"No," he jerked. The Clemenceau no is a quickly jerked grunt. "No, no, I have nothing whatever to say to Canadians."

That ended that. The subject was closed. He smiled again and the talk was back on the friendly between you and me basis.

"Are you ever going to write your personal record and impressions of the war and the treaty as Lloyd George is doing now?" we asked.

"Never," Clemenceau said and smiled at both of us with his eyes. "I am not going back over things. If I tell the truth it will only make too much trouble, too many recriminations, rapprochements — you understand? I am not going back over it."

He smiled off into his own thoughts again and then talked to us as though he were talking to himself. "I made the treaty — there is no use denying that. It doesn't work." He fastened his eyes into mine again. "I know why. But I'm not telling people why. It would only make worse enemies."

He stood up and we walked to the door. Clemenceau never looked out.

"It is nice here, eh?" I looked out at the long line of white beach with a thin surf crisping on it and at the far off green hills. There was a smell of the sea and of rotted kelp. Clemenceau drew a deep breath.

"It's nice here," he said again, then pointed at the big, red banner on the flag pole. "That is the Japanese carp," he explained. "The symbol of virility. They hoist it whenever a male child is born. It is a gift from the wife of the Japanese ambassador."

While we were standing in front of the cottage, another motorcar came up the sand road and turned up the hill. Three men came trudging along through the sand. One of them looked like a florid-faced bookmaker. The other two were satellites and hung back. The bookmaker man, who began to look as though he might be a bartender as he came closer, I recognized.

"Ah, Tardieu," said Clemenceau.

Tardieu greeted us grudgingly.

"My, how many visitors I have," Clemenceau's eyes wrinkled. "What popularity."

All this in French. Tardieu, former French High Commissioner in the U.S., was in a huff. He is Clemenceau's Lieutenant and the Tiger, who is sharpening his claws, had evidently commanded his presence. Clemenceau was enjoying it thoroughly.

Tardieu — "I don't think much of the hospitality of your town. We got in at midnight and had to go to six hotels and none of them would let us in at that hour."

Clemenceau: "Ah. That is respectability."

Tardieu: "No. I told them I was a deputy."

Clemenceau: "Oh you should never have done that. We are not fond of parliamentarians in the Vendee."

Tardieu nursed his grouch and Clemenceau left him standing and walked with us to the gate. He was very charming. "Goodbye Mr. Bird. Goodbye Mr. Hemingway." He said, "perhaps I will see you in Paris in October." He was a very gracious and charming old man and he turned and waved to us as he plodded jerkily back through the sand to where Tardieu was waiting.

It was a 15 mile ride back to the fishing village of Les Sables-D'Ollone through a scrub-oak, sandy, plain where the houses are built close to the ground to avoid the wind and the farmers wage a losing fight against the blowing sand, manuring the ground with kelp hauled from the beach and building windbreaks to keep the encroaching sand out of their gardens. At Les Sables it rained, there was a typewriter and nothing to do until the next train 18 hours away. So I thought about Clemenceau. How did this Clemenceau differ from other men? How did he get to be the Tiger of France?

Because of his Asiatic face, many French scientists believe that he is a descendant of Attila's soldiers, some of whom settled in the Vendee after the Huns were routed in 451.

During the days of the second empire he was arrested and imprisoned for preaching republicanism. He went to America in his youth and followed the Union army as a physician. Later taught French in an American girls' school. Married an American, Miss Mary Plummer.

In the storm of the Commune he returned to Paris and became Mayor of Montmartre, the active leader of the wild element that has given the Butte Montmartre its strange reputation. During the short time he was Mayor, two generals were shot by the Montmartre mob.

Charged into politics and became known as "destroyer of ministries." Became a newspaper editor and wrote several philosophical novels. Attacked President Poincaire venomously within a month after Poincaire's election. Drove Briand from office as Premier. Was appointed Premier under Poincaire's presidency and saved France and perhaps the world.

He carries in his back the bullet fired by Cottin, an insane young radical after the Armistice. He made his first final retirement from public office in 1893 and is said to have destroyed 18 French ministries.

The last time he took office as Premier was when France was "bled white," when the fighting spirit of the troops were exhausted, after a serious mutiny had occurred, and when a peace was being negotiated that would have meant German domination of the world.

Immediately before he made himself Premier, women were parading the streets of Paris with banners reading, "Bring Back Our Soldiers." The French had failed in a ghastly offensive in the Champagne that had turned into a butchery. Morale could have been no lower.

Aristide Briand, the Premier, was said to have received secret offers of peace from Germany — and about to accept them. It looked as though France was done for.

Then came Clemenceau. He knew the Germans. In 1893, after the Casablanca incident he had said, "There will be no apology when Germany had demanded one. There was no apology. And there was to be no defeatist peace now."

Clemenceau came charging out of his retreat. He drove Briand and the others out of power, bucked up the French morale, and put the French into a state of mind where there was no longer any possibility of quitting.

Day after day Clemenceau visited the front, getting in touch with the soldiers. He made short, vigorous talks to the men and thousands of men have seen him under shell fire. Few people are aware how close he once came to being captured by the Germans. In 1918, he was still in a French village when the Germans entered in and had to be hidden away and later smuggled out by loyal French civilians.

Back of the lines, in Paris, at munition factories, in all centres the old tiger visited and became to the people the symbol of a France unconquerable. Then came the long strain of the Peace Conference and his serious wounding by an assassin. People said the old man was failing. His leathery skin was yellower than ever. The combinations of political groups that he had fought and defeated in his career formed a coalition and elected Deschanel for President of France, the position that belonged to Clemenceau if any ever did. He retired from public life and went on a shooting trip to Africa and India.

He came back and went into retirement at his little place on the wild coast of the Vendee where I interviewed him. His health is back, he says he never felt better, and he is beginning to prepare, many people believe, for a political comeback. The Poincaire faction fear him more now than they ever did and they are shaking in their boots.

If Clemenceau's American tour is successful and a triumph, and the Poincaire group have no way out of giving it every aid, the Tiger may come sweeping back into power again. He says he knows why the Versailles treaty does not work. And he should. He made it. And that statement is a powerful weapon to wield on Poincaire who has proved that he cannot work the treaty.

It has been said of Clemenceau that France is his only remaining illusion. He is going to America now, alone, the only free man in Europe, to defend France. And if he decides that it is necessary for him, on his return, to become Premier in order to defend France better — he will be the next Premier.

Meantime, he stands and looks out at the surf curling along his beach, at his great red fish blowing in the wind at the top of the slim white pole, at the red sails of the fishing boats far out on the sea beating up from the coast of Spain toward the very pleasant land of France and he says — "it is a nice place — this. I was born near here, you know. No. Not here. A little further up the coast."

Across from the Post Office

This fragment of a European dispatch was written while Hemingway served as a Star *foreign correspondent, touring the occupied Ruhr district in the spring of 1923. It was never published. The typescript was found in JFK Library.*

Across from the post office in the hot sun of the village square two four-horse coaches packed with boys were drawn up in the midst of a crowd of men. Mothers had said goodbye when they left the house. Fathers and friends were there to see them off.

Some of the boys were sitting back in the coach bashfully. Some were puffing cigarettes defiantly. One kid with a celluloid collar and a pimply face was on the front seat with the driver cutting up. The town smart alec. He had his greatest audience but no one was paying any attention to him. A boy jumped down from the coach straight through the crowd and threw his arms around his father. They walked off with their arms around each other and were back in a moment, the boy climbing back into the coach looking straight ahead and blubbering. A girl on the edge of the crowd was crying and wiping her eyes with her apron. Her brother waved at her.

A third coach drove up. The first two started with cracking whips, shouts, goodbyes, hand wavings, and a hoarse attempt at a song and were out of sight down the steep Belluno road. It was the departure of the conscripts of the class of 1903, that is all the boys born in the county in that year.

The incident has no importance beyond the fact that it is with these boys that Europe makes war. I mention it merely because it was the start of my trip through Germany, for in the post office I found a cable from the *Star* covered with Italian post marks and limp from resting in those wire, unforwarded hotel letter racks that are the ports of all the missing telegrams in the world. It was a full rate, forty-four word cablegram and it had taken fifteen days to come 800 miles from Paris by the hotel forwarding route.

In the extremely courteous language that is employed by managing editors and battalion commanders it requested me to go into Germany from the south pass along the length of the occupation from Offenburg in the Black Forest, down the Rhine towns, through the Ruhr and wherever else necessary and write a series of articles giving the facts on what is happening in this struggle between the French and the Germans, what is behind it, the humorous side of it, if there is any, the real conditions in Germany, the chances of a German collapse and what such a collapse would actually be, in short the cold dope on the whole situation, not written to prove anything or to uphold any policy but simply as an impartial observer. The articles are to be mailed in order to avoid the telegraphic censorship that is practiced by both French and Germans.

So this old, black, hard-boiled, smooth-running typewriter that has chronicled the rise of Mussolini and the fall of Carpentier, the rise of Mustapha Kemal and the fall of Lloyd George, the rise of Poincaire and the execution of Landru and will some day click out the fall of Mussolini, Poincaire and Dempsey has been unfolded and set going greatly to the delight of the four Italian children who with their mother, father, nurse, two traveling salesmen, half a ton of luggage and a solid wave of garlic share this compartment on the Trieste-Paris express with me.

Two Revolutions Are Likely
If Germany Suffers Collapse

This article, adapted from a letter Hemingway wrote while serving as a European correspondent, appeared without a byline in the Star *of March 7, 1923. Hemingway preserved the clipping in his scrapbook.*

You ask about the relation between the standard of living in a country and in inflation of its currency. Well the franc has recently dropped from about twelve to the dollar to about seventeen to the dollar. There has been no rise in the price of living beyond a local rise of five centimes a kilo in the price of bread in Paris. Prices are the same. The reason is that the people still have absolute confidence in their money.

When in 1919 the franc fell rapidly, and without precedent, from about eight to the dollar to seventeen to the dollar, the people became frightened, imports tripled in cost, and everything jumped way up in price. The prices have never come down, except infinitesimally, since then. Wages, salaries, work up toward the prices, but the prices do not come down. It is a matter of confidence.

Inflation in Germany

In Germany where the inflation has been so great, prices in the cities jump each day with the rise of the dollar. Wages jump almost each week. Then when, as recently, the government dumped big stocks of foreign currencies on the market and strengthened the mark, the prices stay up because the merchants have seen money that they take in return for goods sold getting worthless on their hands and will not lower their prices. They are afraid of the next fall of the mark.

Employers lower wages and the government passes laws fixing prices. But it cannot enforce price fixing laws until it can guarantee that the money will not fall again.

Inflation benefits the manufacturers who are able to sell abroad and get pounds sterling, dollars or South American currency for their products and at the same time pay their labor in worthless currency. Inflation appears to benefit the workman because he is employed and gets good big wages which rise as the currency falls. Inflation ruins the teacher, the professional man, the pensioned widow, any bond holders or people with fixed incomes. It also renders it impossible for the worker to save as the money becomes worth-less.

As for the experts, the "world domination" experts and the "complete collapse" experts, they can prove anything. After you see the experts of both sides filing into a room with the brief cases and their pipes and their absolutely, opposing, you're-a-liar array of facts at one of these conferences you get a sort of slant on them.

How France is Dominated

It looks to me about like this: Germany and France have either been at war or preparing for war or recovering from war for some hundreds of years. Germany took Alsace and Lorraine from France in 1870, but France took them from Germany two hundred years before.

France just now, is dominated by a group of fervent, patriotic militarists and a ring of big industrialists headed by the Comite Des Forges or French Steel Trust. The present chamber of deputies was elected in 1918 to serve six years. It is the famous bloc national.

There is a vigorous and numerically small opposition by the communists headed by Marcel Cashin, editor headed by Caillaux, the former prime minister, and ablest financier, who was in prison and his party in disgrace at the time the wartime chamber, that is still dominating France, was elected.

That is, in a broad way, the present French line-up. Of course, there are minor things like the Royalists, headed by Leon Daudet, whose newspaper L'Action Francaise is always being dragged off the Montmartre news stands by the gay young communists and whose newsboys spend most of their time running up alleys with the rougher element in close pursuit.

Berlin Ruled by Industrialists

The German government is in the hands of industrialists who are, as the experts point out, getting very rich. It is in form mildly socialistic, but it is a business man's government, run by business men for the benefit of business men. It has succeeded in making a small group of men enormously rich, they have cached their profits abroad and while they have been taking the profits, the country has been in a sort of producing fever of false prosperity.

Now come the French and virtually declare war on this government. Before the war four-fifths of the German's coal came from Upper Silesia, the Saar and the Ruhr, with the greatest part from the Ruhr. She is now reduced to her one-fifth left, that produced by Saxony. She has lost the iron of Lorraine.

As long as she had the Ruhr she could get along as an industrial nation. Take away the Ruhr and she is through. That is where the "complete collapse" experts come in.

What Complete Collapse Would Mean

Now as to what the complete collapse would mean, we can only figure. We have two cases of complete collapse of currency. Bolshevik Russia deliberately ruined her money in order to destroy her money-holding people, that is all those who were non-producers. She wiped out her middle class and her aristocracy that way by making the rouble valueless through printing million rouble notes on wrapping paper and issuing them on a par with all her other money. After the communists ruined the money and the country in order to destroy the "bourgeois" and start a new society of workers and peasants they found they had to have money to deal with the outside world and among themselves and issued Soviet roubles, which are on a gold basis.

Austria collapsed when she was shorn of her lands and her rich industrial centres and left nothing but a capital and a lot of elegant scenery. When she needed money she printed it and the collapse came when there was no longer anyone who would exchange good money for this printing press money, i.e., when Austrian kronen were no longer quoted on the foreign exchange markets of Paris, London or New York at any price.

Now the powers have gotten together to loan Austria some money and put her on her feet.

Two Revolutions Likely

That is what the complete collapse of Germany would mean, that her money would no longer be quoted on the various exchanges. That is the logical end of the printing press coining. But what would accompany that collapse is what concerns us. We've seen the militarists of Germany overthrown and the next people to go are the industrialists like Stinnes and Thyssen. The Ruhr is the reddest part of Germany. Just now the people are backing the government in a patriotic fervor but I think that if a real collapse comes it will consist of two revolutions; a Red revolution in industrial Germany and a Monarchist revolution in Bavaria. The latter has been on the point of coming off a half dozen times. It is organized as perfectly and carefully and as fully armed as the Fascist movement and is a certainty sooner or later.

Well, the whole thing is much too complicated for a letter.

Offer Sir Donald Soviet Railroads

On his first day back in the job after returning from Europe to become a Daily Star *staff reporter, Hemingway wrote this article, which was published September 10, 1923, without a byline. He saved the clipping in his scrapbook.*

"Canadian capital is as safe to-day in Russia as in Canada," Sir Donald Mann, one of Canada's railway builders told the *Star* to-day on his return to Toronto from a 2,500 mile trip through Soviet Russia.

"I believe the Russian government will live up to any contracts they make. It is vital to them now. They must have foreign capital and they must keep their bargains to get it."

"Did you do any business with the Soviet government?" the *Star* asked Sir Donald.

"They offered me a great many things including the railways," Sir Donald said, settling back in his big office chair. "But I told them no one had any money for railways. Especially as far away as Russia.

"I don't remember the names of all the big men I talked to," Sir Donald continued.

"Did you see Krassin?" he was asked, referring to Leonid Krassin, Bolshevist commissar for trade.

"Yes," Sir Donald said. "It was a big relief to talk to him because he spoke English. I think I met Tchicherin, but I don't remember. I've got a list of them all somewhere."

"Do you mean you were offered the concession of all the Russian railways?" Sir Donald was asked.

"Well you know how it is. They have a list of all these things. Mines, big plants, railways. I had one interview with the government men that lasted six and a half hours. But I didn't do any business with them."

Harvest is Fair

Living in Russia, according to Sir Donald, is fairly comfortable. He traveled from Petrograd to Moscow and from Moscow to the Black Sea.

"In the north they are raising rye and in the south you travel for days through great wheat fields. Crops in the north have been damaged by heavy rains but in the south the harvest is very fair."

"What I was impressed by most," Sir Donald said, "was the earnestness of the people. Men in government positions often work all night. Everyone is working at top speed to get the country back on its feet.

"Moscow is in process of reconstruction. Smashed houses are being rebuilt. New stores are going up every day. There are miles of new shops in Moscow. These shops are all leased by the government to the shop owners."

"Was the Red army much in evidence?" the *Star* asked.

"I didn't see many soldiers," Sir Donald said. "No more than in France. The soldiers were all in khaki. I didn't see any red on their uniform, except the officers had red trimmings."

"I liked the people and the country," Sir Donald continued. "The people were all very kindly and nice to get along with. Of course, there was no French cooking, but you could always get a chop or a steak, sometimes chicken, sometimes ice cream for dessert. The food was good and plain."

"How about liquor?" the reporter asked.

"They drink the native wine, but it has no kick in it. There was no alcohol and no cigars. Everybody smokes cigarets."

"Do the women smoke as much as the men?" asked the reporter.

"Most of them smoke. I didn't meet more than

four or five women. Most of them smoked cigarets. Some didn't though." Sir Donald drew in a deep puff on his own cigar and blew out a cloud of smoke that it would have taken a couple of boxes of Russian cigarets to produce.

On his trip through Russia Sir Donald was accompanied by an Englishman named Wright who acted as interpreter. Mr. Wright was formerly on the staff of the *Winnipeg Free Press*.

"What do you think about the recognition of the Russian Soviet government?" the *Star* asked Sir Donald.

"There is nothing for the powers to do except recognize Russia," Sir Donald said with emphasis. "There is nobody to take the place of the present government. Everyone in Russia tells you that, including the people. They don't want the landed gentry back. They ran away when the revolution came on and left the people to fight. Now they have this present government and I believe it is solid and will last."

"How did you find the railroads and traveling conditions generally?" asked the *Star*.

"I found it much easier to travel in Russia and in Poland than in Germany. The trains were regular and you always had a seat. In Germany I had to stand up, and you never saw such crowding and jamming. A fever of traveling seems to have hit the people.

"They are doing business on a gold basis in Russia and you always know where you are with the money. Their gold notes are worth five to the pound sterling. When you go out to the the the country, or at any time, you can take them to a bank and get English pounds or American dollars for them."

Moscow, according to Sir Donald Mann, is full of American concession hunters. "All out for something for nothing."

Escaped Kingston Convicts
Still at Large

No sooner had Hemingway arrived in Toronto to take up a staff reporter job than assistant managing editor Harry Hindmarsh sent him to Kingston, Ontario, to cover the jail break of gangster Red Ryan and three other cons. (Ryan would go on to become of Canada's most notorious mobsters until shot to death by police in 1936.) Although Hemingway's account received prime front-page play on September 11, 1923, he was not given a byline. This was the start of what was known as "the Hindmarsh treatment" (see page 160 for more). Hemingway's train ticket to Kingston, his handwritten notes for this and three other Kingston articles, plus the clippings themselves, are among his papers in the Hemingway Collection.

Special to the *Star* by a Staff Reporter.

Kingston Mills, Sept. 11. — With four of the five convicts who made a sensational escape from the penitentiary yesterday still at large this morning arrangements are being made to secure bloodhounds to assist in the search. Word was also received this morning from W.S. Hughson, inspector of penitentiaries, that a reward of $50 will be paid for the capture of each of the escaped convicts.

The four men still at large, and who are believed to be hiding in the bush and swamp between the Perth road and the Cataraqui river towards Kingston Mills, are:

Gordon Simpson, Toronto, serving ten years for robbery.

Arthur Brown, Toronto, serving ten years for highway robbery.

Patrick Ryan, alias Norman Slade, Hamilton, sentenced to 25 years and lashes for bank robbery.

Thomas Bryans, Montreal, serving ten years for manslaughter.

Edward McMullen, serving fourteen years for robbing a bank at Wyoming, Ontario, also escaped, but was recaptured three miles from prison, weak with the loss of blood from a gunshot wound in the hand, received from a guard who fired on the party as they escaped.

Guards Out All Night

This morning the guards had been out all night. They were cold and hungry. Farmers were driving in to the town or working in the fields. There were no posses. Everyone in the countryside seemed content to leave the job of man-hunting to the professional man-hunters. The guards completely surrounded the entire woods and were especially thick along the east side to prevent the criminals from breaking across the main road and getting into the woods along the Rideau river. From there they might make their way north and be able to get food at the lumber camps. Everyone was cold and hungry, but there was news.

Last night about eleven o'clock on the narrow muddy road overgrown with underbrush that divides the seven hundred acres of bush into a north and south half, four guards and a scout on horseback were stationed. It was so dark the scout could not see his horse's head. But he heard the fence wires on the south side of the road creak. He shouted to the guards who were further down the road and then there was silence. The four men had their rifles ready.

Then in the dark there was a rush across the road. The guards fired into the dark at the sound and rushed forward. In the dark a man's voice said: "Are you hurt, shorty?" The guards shot again where the voice came from and one of them fired point blank as a man rushed by him toward the north side of the road. The men had crossed from the south tract of the woods to the northern half of the seven hundred acres. About fifteen rifle shots were fired in the dark. There is no blood and there are no bodies.

Found Heavy Wrench

When the sun came up this morning the guards found a hammer and a heavy wrench that the men had dropped when they were fired on while crossing the road. These were taken from Thompson's car and had been taken as weapons when they fled into the woods. A few yards further up the road was a prisoner's cap, one of those gray-blue Sherlock Holmes shaped caps that all the prisoners wear.

I went over the ground where the shooting occurred with Warden Ponsford this morning. He had nothing to say for publication but is confident that all the men crossed into the northern tract during the night, although the guards say they think there were only three.

Warden Ponsford would not say whether the battery of R.C.M.A. at Kingston would be called out to put a tight cordon around the woods while the sixty prison guards, who all know the men by sight and are especially trained in this sort of work, advance in a tightening ring and beat the woods for the convicts. There will be an advance, probably of this kind, some time to-day.

Trace of Man Seen

About nine o'clock word was brought to the warden

by one of the guards patrolling the northern fron-
tier of the woods that traces of one man had been
found where he had climbed over a fence along
the road that bounds the woods on the north. There
was also an unconfirmed report that a farmer had
seen one or two men crossing the road early this
morning. If the men escape out of the north end
of the woods it will be a long chase. There are
several cheese factories a mile or so north of the
present isolated territory, where it is believed the
men will try and get food if they break through.
They have had nothing since early yesterday
morning.

It became known to-day that a long-term convict, who was stationed on duty in the stable, which
was set on fire by the five desperadoes to screen
their bid for liberty, endeavored to foil the attempt
of the five men to escape. When he tried to stop
them in their desperate work, this convict was
roughly handled, and when he persisted in his attempt to frustrate their plans, he was tied up with
a rope inside the building and had it not been for
the quick work of another convict, who found him
and released him, he would have been burned to
death. It is understood that the action of this convict will be brought to the attention of the department of justice.

McMullen is regarded as the ring-leader in the
escape. He and Slade were regarded as two of the
worst convicts in the prison and both have been

closely guarded since they were brought to the penitentiary as it was feared they would plot a getaway. It is believed that the five men had been planning their method of escape for some time.

Plans Went Awry

When back in the penitentiary McMullen stated that the plans for their escape had not worked out as they expected. He said that they figured that after they got over the prison walls they would be able to secure a high powered car from in front of the home of Mrs. H.W. Richardson, who lives close by the prison, and that they would be able to make a quick get-away. McMullen said that he understood that Mrs. Richardson was a millionaire and that he was sure that the car would be close at hand for their use. When they could not get a high powered car they were glad to take a Chevrolet car that was near, but in this they were unable to make the speed they desired.

The capture of McMullen was due to the fact that he was weak from loss of blood from a shot he had received in the left hand from a revolver in the hands of Guard Allan, who chased the fleeing convicts in an automobile. When the convicts ran their car into a gateway, near Kemp's farm, about three miles from this city, and made for the woods close by, McMullen had to drop out of the flight and was found lying on the ground alongside a fence near the road about one hundred feet from the car. He was unarmed and as a result of his weakened condition he was not able to put up any fight. He declared to the guards who surrounded him that if he had not been shot they would never have taken him alive.

McMullen is now confined to the hospital at the penitentiary, but it is stated that his condition is not regarded as at all serious. The shot from the revolver went through his index finger.

It was at ten o'clock yesterday morning that a great cloud of thick, yellow-white smoke began to pour from the barn just inside the east wall of the penitentiary. It was the thick dense smoke of a burning straw stack and as it rose it cut off the view of the guard standing with his rifle in the watchtower overlooking the burning barn.

Five men, in the gray prison clothes, ran out of the barn toward the twenty-foot, steep wall. One of them carried a long two-by-four in which spikes had been driven at intervals. The fat man carrying the long scantling leaned it against the wall and a slim kid, his prison cap pulled down over his eyes, swarmed up it to the top of the wall. He carried a length of rope, which he fastened to the end of the scantling. He made the rope fast and then slid down the other side of the wall.

A big husky with a heavy under-shot jaw followed him over. On his heels came a little runt who scrambled up the scantling like a monkey. He was followed by a thick set, ham-faced man who scrambled awkwardly over the wall.

Standing at the foot of the scantling while they all went up was a thick, freckle-faced man whose prison cap could not hide his flaming head. It was "Red" Ryan. The others who had climbed over were Young Brown, Big Simpson, Runty Bryans and Wyoming McMullen.

As "Red" Ryan started up the ladder, Matt Walsh, chief keeper of Portsmouth penitentiary, came running around the corner to see the burning barn. Walsh saw "Red" on the ladder and ran toward the scantling to try and jerk it down, shouting the alarm as he ran. "Red" saw him coming, realized that he was trapped, and came down the ladder. He had left a pitchfork leaning against the jail wall for just this emergency.

As Walsh reached the ladder "Red" reached for the pitchfork. Walsh tackled him and "Red" swung with all his might on Walsh's head with the pitchfork. Walsh went down and "Red" dropped the fork and went up the scantling and over the wall.

The men were strung out across the field outside the prison wall running for Mrs. Richardson's house where a car was standing. The guard in the tower was still cut off by the thick smoke. Allan Forsythe, the only other guard in sight, thought that he could stop them without shooting. He had dropped over the wall and was just behind the run-

ning men. He had never shot anyone and something
held him back from beginning. He shouted at the
men but they kept on going.

The Guard Shoots

As they climbed into the little Chevrolet car belonging to "Shorty" Thompson, who was doing a
painting job at Richardson's, Allan Forsythe com-
menced shooting. He couldn't tell what his shots
did, but he was sure he had hit someone. The Chevrolet kept on going. Forsythe stopped a car that
was passing and stepped out after the car careering
wildly ahead up the road.

McMullen was at the wheel of the Chevrolet –
that is, he was hunched over what was left of the
wheel. One of Forsythe's shots had cut the wheel
clean in two and smashed McMullen's left hand.
He drove on with his right hand, hunched low, his
face paling from the amount of blood he was losing. The other two big men were in the back of
the car with "Young" Brown, the wild kid. On the
front seat with McMullen sat "Runty" Bryans. One
of Forsythe's bullets ripped through the back of
the car and out the front above "Runty's" head.
It would have hit a full sized man in the skull.

A Wild Chase

Back of the little car was strung out a wild chase.
All sorts of cars had been commandeered in Kingston. As the little motor car went along the road

from the penitentiary, through the streets of Kingston and north on the Inverary road, the cars behind kept gaining. Directly behind was the Ford
commandeered by Forsythe who kept on firing.
The prisoners' car was going along a narrow strip
of asphalt road with houses and cottages on either
side. It looked as though any minute they might
be overtaken. There was no cover on either side.

Then the road widened out into country stone
road. The houses fell away. They crossed the two
railway tracks of the Canadian Pacific and Canadian National, dipped down a long hill, past a
quarry on the left, and were in farming and bush
country. On the right they were passing a long
stretch of thick, hardwood timber, the trees just
going yellow and red in the fall. On the top of
the hill they could see it stretched out for miles
ahead. The men looking out behind could see that
they had a lead of about two hundred and fifty
yards on the nearest of the pursuing cars.

McMullen turned the car sharply to the left and
ran it down the bank into a sunken field. The convicts ripped off the seats, grabbed the tool bags,
the tire pump and jack, climbed the bank and cut
across the Inverary road into the woods. As the
last man was going into the woods Forsythe came
up in his Ford. But his cartridges were gone.

There are seven hundred acres in the patch of
woods the convicts are hiding in. It is bounded
by roads on all sides and is surrounded by prison

guards armed with rifles. Across the middle of the patch of woods runs a narrow, muddy road, over-hung with trees.

McMullen Captured

Last night at about six-thirty, Warden Ponsford, who is in charge of the pursuit, found McMullen about forty yards from where the men entered the McAdoo's Woods. The warden, a kindly-looking gray-mustached man in a gray suit, felt hat and worried look in his eyes, was going over the route the men had taken into the woods when he saw a blue shirt lying under a low growing cedar. He thought it meant that one of the men was discarding his prison clothes and bent down to look. It was McMullen, white from loss of blood, lying under the little cedar, his shirt pulled over his head and his legs and shoes covered with grass.

Warden Ponsford pulled McMullen to his feet and called a patrol. Surrounded by twelve guards with rifles, McMullen was white and shaky. "I'm through," he said, "leave me alone." His hand was still bleeding.

One of the guards said: "Well, are you going to try and run, McMullen?" McMullen looked at the twelve rifle barrels: "What do you think I wanta do? Commit suicide?" They took him in a motor car back to the penitentiary over the same road he had driven in the morning. He was very quiet.

Stewart Patterson, one of Warden Ponsford's lieutenants in the man hunt, said the search parties must have passed McMullen twenty times as he lay there. The cover in the wood is so dense a man cannot make his way through it in places.

Matt Walsh, the head keeper, who was beaten up with a pitchfork by "Red" Ryan, is not seriously injured, although badly marked. He is commanding a detachment in the hunt. "I am leaving now to return to the woods where the men are believed to be cornered and where the closing in on them is due to start," he said to-day.

Gordon Simpson was serving a ten year term following his conviction in Hamilton, Toronto and Guelph for a series of robberies which he participated in, headed by the notorious Tommy Quinn, now serving ten years in Kingston, too, along with several others of the gang. Following his arrest after a large number of shopbreakings in Hamilton, Toronto, and throughout the province, Simpson was taken to Hamilton for trial, and on February 4, 1921, was sentenced to six years for shopbreaking and theft of cloth. Then he was brought to Toronto and sentenced on February 18, 1921, on five charges of shopbreaking and theft, and received a five-year sentence on each charge, the sentences to run concurrently.

Lord and Lady Cranworth

While he was suffering the "Hindmarsh treatment" in the fall of 1923, Hemingway was handed many menial assignments usually reserved for the most inexperienced apprentice reporters. Junior reporters were often asked to go over to luxury hotels, such as Toronto's King Edward Hotel, to see if any notable guests had arrived. That is likely how Hemingway came to write this September 1923 article, which he saved in his scrapbook.

Latest of many arrivals from the Old Land, of British aristocracy, at present in Toronto at the King Edward, are Lord and Lady Cranworth on their first trip to Canada and the United States. They are accompanied by Major Buxton and the latter's nephew, E. Barnes.

Lord and Lady Cranworth arrived at Quebec Sept. 22, and will be on this continent for three months.

Tall, with stately presence, typical English coloring and blue-gray eyes and curling brown hair, Lady Cranworth said: "We loved Quebec. Yes, we were in New York; I didn't like it so well as Canada. I think what has impressed me most so far is the coloring. Your trees are wonderful. We are going to Winnipeg and on through to the Coast." Lord Cranworth, tall and dark, with moustache, stated: "We are out here on business first, mixed with pleasure." The party stated they were motoring out this morning 12 miles in the country for a game of golf.

Lord Cranworth, eldest son of the first Baron Cranworth, was educated at Eton and Trinity College, Cambridge, and served in the South African War 1900-1; B. E. Africa, 1906-11; France and East Africa, 1915-18. He won the M.O. and French Croix de Guerre and was twice mentioned in despatches. He has the works, "A Colony in the Making," and "Profit and Sport in British East Africa," to his credit. The party will be in Toronto until Thursday.

On the Golf Course with Lloyd George

While covering David Lloyd George's arrival in New York in October 1923, Hemingway followed the former British Prime Minister everywhere — even onto the golf course, as recorded in this unpublished dispatch. In his first two days on assignment he wrote ten stories about Lloyd George, but two — including this one and Appendix 17 — were spiked by editors and have never before been published. For more details see page 181.

The *Star* was the only newspaper present when Lloyd George and J.W. McConnell defeated General Sir Arthur Currie and J.J. McGill in the first golf game played by the former Prime Minister on the American Continent and the third he has played in over a year. Lloyd George left the Mount Royal Hotel in a limousine belonging to Mr. J. W.

McConnell this morning at 10 o'clock. With him were the other members of the golfing party. Lloyd George was not dressed in golfing clothes but wore a blue serge lounge suit and a grey soft hat. At the Royal Montreal Club Lloyd George proved he is no dub golfer. He is simply out of practice. He has tremendous possibilities and several times made shots especially with his mashie that were reminiscent of Jock Hutchison but his wooden clubs were a mess. At the start he was lucky to get sixty yards from the tee, topping the ball being his great failing. He stuck to his wood though and on the long seventeenth made a siege gun drive that went like a six-inch shell projectory charge almost two hundred yards straight down in the fairway. His putting was average.

The *Star* saw the first six holes from a distance. The seventh was won by L.G. eight to eleven. Sir Arthur Currie getting into bad trouble at the railway track. Lloyd George pitched over the railway track onto the green. Currie finally wafted a mashie shot over the track and there was some very bad putting. Lloyd George had not yet struck his game. The ninth hole L.G. drove into a bunker. J.J. McGill drove well. W.J. McConnell pitched out with a mashie. Currie's mid iron shot went into the bunker. L.Gs mashie shot dropped into the sand pit. McGill pitched onto the green. McConnell's mashie shot was on the green from the sand trap. Sir Arthur overran his putt. L.G's putt was short.

McGill overran the cup. McConnell's putt lipped the hole. McGill sank his putt. Currie's hole seven and eight.

Tenth hole. Currie drove long and straight down the fairway one hundred and fifty yards. McConnell shot a long high one of seventy-five yards with a pronounced hook. McGill played a mid iron one hundred yards. L.Gs mid iron shot was good for another hundred. Sir Arthur dropped a mashie into the sand trap. McConnell cleared the bunker with a mashie shot and was in the trap on the far side of the green. McGill was on the green with a mashie shot out of the bunker. L.G. played out of the trap onto the green with a corking mashie shot. McConnell sank his putt. McGill's putt also dropped. It was L.G's hole, three up.

On the short eleventh hole McGill drove well straight down the fairway. L.G. lofted one about forty yards into the sand trap. McConnell played a beautiful mashie shot to the edge of the green. L.G. putted from the extreme edge of the green to within six inches of the cup. Sir Arthur's putt overran the cup. McGill missed this putt. It was L.G's hole four and three.

Twelfth hole. Currie drove a beauty down the right side of the course. "What a beauty. Nothing the matter with that one except you can't quite use your brassie with it," L.G. said admiringly. McConnell drove a screecher straight down the fairway. "That evens us up General," L.G. said. McGill played a mid iron. Currie a beautiful brassie. L.G. produced one of his corking mashie shots over the bunker. McGill's putt was long about eight yards. McConnell putted dead to the pin. Currie's putt was on the riff of the cup. L.G. sunk an eight-incher for the hole five and four.

Thirteenth hole. L.G. made a corking drive. McGill lunged with his drive and hooked. L.G's ball was in the trap and McConnell lofted it out. Currie sent a beautiful brassie shot. L.G. topped a brassie. He was having no luck with his wooden clubs. "I've had only two games in the last twelve months," he said. McConnell was on the green with a mashie. McGill the same. Currie putted and nearly sunk a thirty footer. L.G's putt ran two feet beyond the hole. McConnell sunk his putt for a six. McGill missed. Six a piece on the hole. "What is your score, sir?" "Shh," Lloyd George whispered, "We're two up and five to play." The *Star* rushed to the telephone in the Club House.

Lloyd George the Great Survivor

Hemingway bombarded the Star *with articles while covering former British prime minister Lloyd George's arrival in New York for a cross-Canada tour (see page 181 for more details). This story was not published.*

He is the only one of the four men who sat around a table at Versailles to remake the world who survived. Where are the other men who sat with him?

Woodrow Wilson, a broken man, his aims unaccomplished and his accomplishments repudiated.

Clemenceau, a bitter and disillusioned old man, living in a little cottage on a desolate strip of the sandy Vendee coast alone with his hates.

Orlando, a voiceless politician in a country that has abandoned parliamentary government. All of them alone. All of them bitter.

But today — description of L.G. arriving hearty, healthy, cheerful, handsome, etc.

It was Lloyd George, the great survivor.

He has been spared for something. Perhaps it is to save the world. He tried that once at an old seaport town called Genoa. All the Nations who hate each other met and sat down at table together. When they snarled and refused to discuss, Lloyd George calmed them and brought them together. When France or Russia threatened to go away Lloyd George talked and they stayed.

I heard him talk there in times of crisis and he was very wonderful. But he couldn't stay. He had to get back to London and finally the "ship of Genoa" as he always called it, went on the rocks and all the nations went away.

They say that Genoa and the Near East gave him his death blow in Politics. But talking with him on the Mauritania today I could see that nothing could ever give him a death blow.

Genoa was a tragic conference. The last of the great conferences. Of the men who sat with Lloyd George there, Walter Rathenau, cold and idealistic, was shot in the back in his own motor car as he drove to the Foreign Office in Berlin.

Vorovsky, the Russian, scholarly and kindly, was murdered at table as he drank his after dinner coffee in a hotel in Lausanne.

Stambulisky, a roaring bull of a man who worked only for the good of Bulgaria, hunted down and killed in a field by his own soldiers while he tried to hide his fat bulk in a straw stack.

Gounaris, the Greek Premier, was carried from his bed sick with typhoid to meet his death in a drizzling rain in the courtyard of the military hospital.

All this within a year.

But Lloyd George carries not one scar from that conference. He is the great survivor.

There was Northcliffe too. Northcliffe who had been a friend of Lloyd George and then hated him and swore to drive him from office. But Northcliffe was dead and buried before Lloyd George ever relinquished the Premiership.

Now Northcliffe's brother has kept up the feud. But I would watch out if I were that brother. He is not to be killed, nor discredited, nor kept out of the political life that is his existence this Lloyd George.

Fifth Generation of Family Lives On Old Canadian Manor

Hemingway practiced his use of repetition in this human-interest feature (see page 210 for more discussion). It appeared without a byline in the Star *of October 20, 1923. The clipping was saved by Hemingway in his scrapbook.*

Special to the *Star* by a Staff Reporter.

Newmarket, Oct. 20 – This is the story of the old Dawson Manor. It is all mixed up with Indians and Osgoode Hall. With stage coaches and a dark eyed high school girl that lives alone with her grandmother in one of the most beautiful old houses in Canada.

About a mile north of Newmarket, where the long stretch of Yonge Street runs through a rolling country, a big galvanized iron mail box stands beside the road. On one side, carefully rubbed out, but still showing, is the name Emily Fierhelier. On the other side in bright, new, black stencil; Mrs. Emily Dawson.

From the mail box a sandy drive turns up through the flaming maples past a plowed field toward where the warm mellow color of an old brick house shows through the dark pines. The dark pines overshadow the house and there is a green slope of lawn in front. The house itself is built of brick. English ivy climbs beside the door.

There are some beds of asters on the lawn and back of the house a tangle of old orchard. Lilacs are massed at the back and an old brick wall running out to the workmen's kitchen of the old days is built of the same beautifully set, weather softened brick.

Inside the house is dusky. There is no electricity or gas. But it is not gloomy and before the nine-foot-wide fireplace in the dusk sat an old lady, the Mistress of the Manor, who although she lives in Mackenzie King's riding, speaks of the Reformers as "Those rebels," and says, "My grandfather, who built the Manor was a Conservative, and of course I am a Conservative."

She is an altogether charming and delightful whitehaired grandmother and about a month ago at Osgoode Hall had her name changed from Fierhelier back to her girlhood name of Dawson so there would be a Dawson living at the Dawson Manor. Though there was a hint of tragedy, "I had no love for the Fierhelier name," she said evenly and as a matter of fact, "I had to support myself for a long time while my husband was alive."

John Dawson, the grandfather, who was a J.P. in England, built the Manor House. It was started in 1830.

"My grandfather's family started to cross the Atlantic in a sailing vessel. They had chartered three vessels but there was some accident and they had to put back to England. The second time they started they were in a bad storm and landed on the coast of Greenland. But they finally got to New York."

The grand-daughter, Margaret Fierhelier, shy, dark, with great dark eyes, and very much in love with her grandmother had come into the room.

"Margaret stays here with me to keep me company," Mrs. Dawson said. "She is the fifth generation of the Dawson family to live in the old house."

John Dawson, J.P., it seems had four sons. They took four hundred acres on each side of Yonge Street, coming straight to Toronto overland from New York.

"The bridge was finished the year of the rebellion. I've often heard them tell about those days. Two hundred Indians came to the gate down at Yonge Street and offered to fight for the Conservatives. There was much fighting then. Sir Aemilius Irving's father, Captain Irving, was in the fighting between the Conservatives and the Reformers at the bridge over the Holland River near Bradford. Captain Irving's old coachman used to tell us children about the fighting that day."

"Were you born here on the place?" asked the reporter.

"Oh, yes. My father was William Dawson, the third son. I remember in the old days how the stage coaches used to go by on Yonge Street. Yonge Street was young then. But it was even younger when my grandfather came out," Mrs. Dawson answered.

It was quite dark now. Mrs. Dawson brought out some fruit cake carefully wrapped in oiled paper from the sideboard in the great, dusky dining room with the fireplace that could hold almost an entire sawlog.

"It's Christmas cake," she said.

"Enoch Rodgers was the carpenter," Mrs. Dawson said, her mind running back and trying to collect early, half-remembered details in the dusk. "I think that the bricks were burned on the Phillips farm. Once not so long ago I had a mason in to do some work and he said there were enough bricks in each chimney to build an ordinary house nowadays. The floors are two inches thick, of oak."

Mrs. Dawson went upstairs and brought down an enormous flowered waistcoat. It was the sort of waistcoat to go over the chest of a great, well-fed, robust, fox-hunting squire. The material was as good as ever.

"That is my grandfather's vest," she said proudly, knowing that the waistcoat spoke volumes in itself. "You can see that he was a fine, big man."

The waistcoat would have easily surrounded both the reporter and the photographer.

"And will there be a Dawson on the place always?" asked the reporter.

"I don't know. My son has talked some of taking the name of Dawson. But he's moved away, and besides, it is different if you weren't born here. Nobody feels quite the same about it as I do. The first winter I was here there was someone who was going to spend the rest of her days here with me.

Her voice broke a little.

"That was just what happened. She died and I was alone here. But now I have Margaret."

She smiled at Margaret with the quick, confident smile of the old, and Margaret smiled back with the quick, confident smile of the very young.

"Margaret thinks it is pretty far to go to high school, but I tell her it is what we had in our day and the distances haven't changed."

"Is it fun living here in the old house?" the reporter asked Margaret.

"Oh, yes. With grandmother," Margaret said.

Cars Slaying Toronto's Splendid Oak Trees

Cars were killing trees as far back as 1923, according to this story written under the name of Peter Jackson — a pen name used by Hemingway. For more discussion of this article, which is an early example of environmental reporting, see page 209.

By Peter Jackson

A chill, cold wind blows over High Park. There is snow in the air.

Other trees sway with the wind. The pines seem to enjoy it. But the oaks are sullen and rigid. Stripped of their leaves by the wind, they stand stiff and despairing looking against the sky. For the oaks are dying.

They are dying because they cannot stand the city. And the city comes nearer and nearer all the time.

Other trees are built to make compromises with the city. They have special defences against the attacks the city launches against them. But the oak is not built for compromises. It is like some animal of prehistoric times, built only for a certain environment. And when that environment is changed it dies.

Motor cars kill oak trees, declares Dr. C.D. Howe, dean of forestry at the University.

"The dust constantly stirred up by the automobiles settles on the oak leaves and forms a film," Dr. Howe stated. "It is exceedingly fine and often contains oil. The film on the leaves stops the breathing pores and the trees suffocate. They must have air to breathe just as an animal must."

It is because the oak leaf is smooth and offers a perfect surface for the film of dust and the city smoke that the sturdiest of trees succumbs to the city, where the elm and the maple survive, according to Dr. Howe.

"Elm trees have rough leaves with minute little hairs, like a stubbly beard," Dr. Howe told the *Star Weekly*. "The dust particles cannot make a perfect film and cut off the respiration as they do in the oak. So the oaks are being slowly smothered."

Toronto's oaks are dying in Queen's Park as well as in High Park. According to authorities, one reason they are unable to resist the steady smothering of the dust film is because of the weakness of old age.

Most of Toronto's oak trees are close to one hundred years old. At seventy-five to a hundred years an oak tree begins to weaken. In good, rich soil in Canada an oak should live to be 250 or 300 years if it were not exposed to the dust, smoke and gases of the city. In England there have been cases of oaks reaching the age of 600 years. That was in the country.

When the oak has been weakened by the smothering caused by the shutting off of its respiratory organs, the fungus attacks it. The particular type of fungus that kills Toronto's oaks starts in at the roots. It spreads from the roots and gradually rots out the heart. The oak lives on for a time as a shell, its sap mounting in the spring and its leaves struggling against the city's dust assaults, and then dies.

Young trees with the vitality to resist the city's attacks are the one solution if Toronto is to have oaks, according to Dr. Howe.

"I believe I could successfully propagate red and black oaks in Queen's Park," Dr. Howe said. "But they would need adequate protection against the children. Children playing thoughtlessly grab a tree and either hurt the bark or shake the roots. They would need to be fenced around while they were growing."

Pines are even more sensitive to civilization than oaks. All over southern Ontario the pines are sickening from some unknown cause.

"When we don't know what the matter is we say it is climatic or physiological," the forestry dean declared, "just as the physicians ascribe some maladies to the nerves."

The pines and the spruces are dying from some general disability. They, too, like the oaks, breathe through their needles. Like the oak, too, their needles have a flat surface where the dust from the oiled highways can lie in a close, tight, deadly film. Perhaps the pines also are victims of the motor car.

An Absolute Lie, Says Dr. Banting, of Serum Report

In this story, identified as Hemingway's work by William McGeary, Hemingway obtains a rare interview from the publicity shy Dr. Banting, the Toronto scientist who discovered insulin. Banting never gave interviews, but agreed to talk to a Star *man only because another doctor had leaked a report that Banting had discovered a new serum that is "more important than insulin." This article appeared in the* Star *October 11, 1923. Three weeks later Hemingway wrote his father in Oak Park to say he had just interviewed Banting for the* Star.

The report that he has been working on a serum to combat pernicious anemia is absolutely unfounded, Dr. Frederick G. Banting, winner of the Nobel prize on research told the *Star* today.

"It is an absolute lie," Dr. Banting stated. "Ever since the report got around, I have been having letters, telegrams and messages of all sorts coming in on us. The greatest service people could do to us is to leave us alone to work."

Dr. Banting spoke in his usual slow, careful way.

"I feel very badly that Mr. Charles Best was not mentioned in the Nobel award. I am very anxious that it should be known that Mr. Best had an intimate part in the discovery of insulin. I am sure that Mr. Best will feel it too. I am of course going to share the award with him in every way and want everybody to know the part he played. He ought to be back here from Boston on Wednesday.

"I am more than gratified that the award should have come to Canada and to the university but I think it is very important that everyone should give the proper credit to Mr. Best."

Moscow Theatre Company Will Not Come to Toronto

While on assignment as the Star*'s European correspondent, Hemingway made extra money by writing for two rival news services. But the double-dealing did not end when Hemingway returned to Toronto as a staff reporter in the fall of 1923. This clipping, saved in Hemingway's scrapbook, is from the* Globe *of November 27, 1923.*

Any controversy which might possibly have arisen in connection with the appearance in Toronto of the Moscow Art Theatre Company, which is at present playing in New York, has been nipped in the bud through the independent cancellation of the company's Toronto engagement by Lawrence Solman, Manager of the Royal Alexandra Theatre. At the same time local people who had been approached by the management with a view to se-

curing distinguished patronage for the performances were cleared of any suspicion of favoring the
Soviet Government in an interview granted the
Globe by Prof. James Mavor, noted economist,
who was consulted on the matter by those so
approached.

The Moscow Art Theatre Company was billed
for an engagement at the Royal Alexandra Theatre
during Christmas week, but Mr. Solman told the
Globe last night that he had, after due consider-
ation of the matter, insisted upon the cancellation
of the engagement. There were, he said, several
remonstrances from the company, but he stood firm
in his decision. The result is that the Moscow company has abandoned entirely its proposed visit to
Toronto, at the same time canceling performances
scheduled in Montreal.

Mr. Solman explained to the *Globe* that he had
objected to the engagement on the ground that the
Russian plays included in the repertory of the company were not of a character that would be ac-
ceptable during Christmas week, as they were of
a sombre nature. The fact that the dialogue was
in a foreign language, Russian, also made the engagement appear impracticable from a business
standpoint. The engagement was canceled, so far
as Mr. Solman was concerned, entirely on the
ground that it could not be expected to result in
other than a serious financial loss. It was considered unlikely that the people interested in Russian

drama, together with those knowing the Russian language, would be sufficient in number to warrant even one performance.

Prof. Mavor, interviewed last night at his home, said: "The management of the Moscow Art Theatre Company having attempted to form a group of patrons and patronesses in Toronto for the purpose of aiding the company, should a visit to Toronto be decided upon, I was asked to advise on the subject. In case any question might be raised by anyone regarding the affiliations of the Moscow Art Theatre, I suggested that the treasurer of the company be requested to write a letter stating precisely the facts of the case, in order that the committee of patrons and patronesses might be protected against any misinterpretation. So far as I am aware, this letter has not been furnished."

Referring to statements made in the evening papers last night, Prof. Mavor declared that they were quite irrelevant.

"The actors of the Moscow Art Theatre," the professor continued, "are really great artists, and, personally, I have the utmost sympathy with them in the unfortunate position in which they must find themselves. If they are entirely disconnected with the Soviet and the Third International, this can easily be disclosed. But if they are connected with either of these organizations, difficulties were bound to arise for those who were prepared to take a generous interest in them in Toronto.

"The attempt to drag the University of Toronto into this matter," he added, "is absolutely gratuitous, so far as I am aware."

When word of the adverse rumors concerning the company which had arisen in Toronto was communicated to Morris Gest, the producer, the following wire was sent back: "The whole thing is ridiculous. France investigated the Moscow Art Theatre before, and invited them as guests of the country. America did the same. I personally investigated it thoroughly. Positively no foundation for it."

No Room in Canada for European Reds, Preacher Maintains

After the Russian revolution, the influx of "Reds" was big news all over North America, and the threat of a spread of Socialism throughout Europe and even Toronto itself sparked outrage from the pulpit, as Hemingway recorded while assigned to cover a Sunday sermon for the Star *in the fall of 1923. He saved the clipping in his scrapbook. This is the same "Red" paranoia lampooned in Hemingway's humorous sketch, "Red Flag in Toronto" (see Appendix 4).*

Socialists of every ilk were severely and emphatically condemned by Rev. W.R. Mackay of Bond Street Congregational Church in his sermon yesterday evening. His sermon, which advanced brotherly love and the Golden Rule in place of any form of Socialism as the panacea for all this world's ills, was designed expressly as a reply to the group of returning British harvesters who last Sunday visited his church and afterward announced that their visit should be regarded solely in the light of payment for a free meal.

"These men," he said, referring to the harvesters, "have simply shown themselves in a very bad light. I don't know of any worse sin in the world than ingratitude. I did not prepare my sermon, which was based on the story of the prodigal son, for them. I was preaching it to my own prodigals who come here from time to time. That type of men is undesirable, and we do not need the type which bites the hand that feeds them. They claim to be Socialists, and they exemplify the doctrines they profess.

"Socialism," he continued, "is a very difficult thing to define, because there are many varieties of Socialists in the world. It has several different meanings, but I speak tonight to the extreme type using that name. Over in Europe it is today breeding danger and trouble, and everywhere in the world it is creating disturbance."

Socialists, he claimed, were sowing the tares in the wheat fields of mankind. It was being offered, very much as a patent medicine was sometimes offered, as a remedy for every ill, and its exponents could very well be compared with a company of quack doctors. Marxisim had bred a peculiar brand of "made-in-Germany" trouble, which in practice must fall.

"It is true," he said, "that this world is suffering from a variety of ills. But Socialism would tear the old machine to pieces and would abolish all rights of private property. It would stop Capitalism. It would nationalize everything. It would destroy the Church. It is aimed at religion and the home and marriage." The doctrine that all men were equal in every sense was the greatest of fallacies. There were physical differences and mental differences which forever would bar the realization of the Socialists' ideal of equality.

In Toronto itself there were many "Reds." He had talked to them and had listened to them expounding their doctrines. Canada did not want the rubbish of the old lands to come here, since the melting-pot was incapable of assimilating mud with gold.

Not Socialism, in any form, but the Golden Rule, he concluded, was the logical cure for the ills of the world. Mankind must realize the ideal of service and of brotherly love and the world would then find its difficulties vanishing.

She Sacrifices Herself
That Children May Live

Almost every Toronto Star *reporter is asked at one time or another to write an appeal for the* Star's *Santa Claus Fund charity drive, and Hemingway was no exception, writing this before Christmas of 1923. Hemingway thought enough of it to paste it in his scrapbook.*

The woman was crucifying motherhood. Her husband had left her with three small children to provide for. So because they were of her body she was giving her body as a sacrifice to save them from death. She was squandering her own life and health that they might live. She had worked until she had become a shadow. Her big eyes in sunken lids seemed to hold flame as they glowed from the pallid transparency of her thin face. Her lips were colorless. There was not a spare ounce of flesh on her nor a spare gill of blood in her veins. Her bones showed as knobs and hollows in her gaunt cheeks.

She was literally giving her body as a sacrifice for the children's sake.

Not so very long ago, as the years count, she must have been a comely enough girl. Now she looked old and very, very tired. It must have been a very long time since she smiled. A smile now would have been strange on the tragic mask of her face.

But she would never give in. There was no question of her shirking the responsibility of the three children. No word of surrender passed the thin line of her lips.

Yet she realized to the full the bitterness of her burden.

"Often when I go out," she said, "I do not want to come back. I would not if it were not for the children. I wish always that I could waken up and find that it was all just a dream."

She had worked for such a long time. Her husband had apparently never been fond of it. So she had gone out long before he left. She had to earn food for the children.

At present she had a domestic job in the mornings. She earned six dollars a week. How did she manage? She had to pay $2.50 a week for the rent of the room. A woman charged another $1.50 for caring for the children. She had to buy milk. And as she spoke she glanced, as if she were explaining, at the baby sleeping in the little car beside the stove from the open mouth of which the blue flames of the coke leaped with more than a hint of evil fumes.

No, she had not much left for food. But she always got a meal at the house where she worked. That did for her. She was not a big eater. So she was able to spend what money there was on food for the children.

It was strange to look from the mere shred of a woman to the comparatively fat, healthy children whose mother she was. But then she was a small eater. She did not need much. She gave it to the children. She worked for them. She starved for them. She literally indeed gave them of her body. When a woman begins to sacrifice, there is no limit except death. And this woman did not want to die while she could help the children.

If this account of a Toronto home touches you, will you please mail tonight some money to the Star Santa Claus Fund, 18 King Street West, Toronto.

Greatest Boy Actor Is a Toronto Lad

Hemingway quit the Star *staff as of January 1, 1924, but did not leave Toronto until January 12. During his last days in the city, he earned extra travel funds by writing two stories for the Toronto* Mail and Empire, *including this story about a child actor that appeared in January 1924 and was preserved in Hemingway's clipping scrapbook.*

To be judged the best child actor on the continent, in competition with 10,000 stage children from all the dramatic schools of the world; to be awarded a scholarship which will meet his expenses for an extended course of dramatic training at whatever school the boy may decide; to be honored by appearing before President Coolidge and his cabinet in a special performance — these are the honurs which have been bestowed upon a Toronto boy, nine-year-old Breffni Beggs, son of Mr. and Mrs. N. G. Beggs, 6 Jean Street this week.

Breffni, accompanied by his mother, went to New York last week to take part in the competition held by the National Stage Children's Association to decide the greatest boy actor. He was one of 15 selected from the 10,000 who competed, and who yesterday gave a performance before Governor Smith of New York in the Apollo theatre, New York. At the performance the Toronto lad was awarded the scholarship, as evidence of his talent for the stage.

In view of the large number of contestants from all over the world the success of the Toronto boy is more than an ordinary honor and it is, in addition, an honor for Hart House and Director Bertram Forsyth, who trained the Beggs boy for the part of Shylock, in which role he appeared in the contest. He appeared last year at Hart House in a minor role in "Playbills." It is quite possible that some of the training to be given Breffni, under his scholarship, will be given him at Hart House.

Later in the week the 15 principal contestants will appear before President Coolidge and his cabinet at the White House theatre, Washington, D.C.

Marks Not Caused by Ill-Treatment

Hemingway's last act in breaking ties with the Star *was to write for its rivals, first the* Globe *on November 27, 1923, (see Appendix 21) and finally this, the second of two stories for the* Mail and Empire *(which later merged with the* Globe *to form the* Globe and Mail — *still an arch rival of the* Star*). This short report on an inquest into a hanging appeared in the* Mail and Empire *on January 8, 1924 and was apparently Hemingway's last work as a journalist in Toronto.*

Special to the *Mail and Empire*.
Goderich, Ont., Jan. 8. — The Town Hall was crowded to standing room tonight at the adjourned inquest ordered by Coroner Dr. Hunter to inquire into the death of Charles Bulpitt, a "home" boy, aged 16, employed on the farm by B. J. Cox, a

few miles from Goderich. Bulpitt was found hanging by the neck in the barn. Upon examination several marks were found upon the body which led the authorities to believe that the boy had been ill-treated.

Dr. Macklin, who performed the post-mortem, testified that these marks were characteristic of death caused by hanging. The marks did not show any signs of being caused by any hard blows.

Cox was severely cross-questioned for nearly two hours by Crown Attorney Seager, K.C. He admitted whipping the boy frequently with a strap because he did not do as he was told. He could give no reason for the boy's act, admitting that he seemed despondent.

Other evidence as to the life on the farm was given by T. Mathers, who worked for Cox some four years ago. The case has aroused considerable interest throughout the district. Adjournment was made till Wednesday, Jan. 16.

NOTES

PROLOGUE
Ticket to Toronto, 1919

1. Ernest Hemingway to James Gamble, March 3, 1919, Carlos Baker, *Ernest Hemingway: Selected Letters* (New York: Charles Scribner's Sons, 1981), pg. 21.
2. EH to Lawrence T. Barnett, April 30, 1919, Baker, *Selected Letters*, pg. 23.
3. EH to Gamble, Baker, *Selected Letters*, pg. 21.
4. EH to Howell Jenkins, December 20, 1919, Baker, *Selected Letters*, pg. 29.
5. EH to Bill Smith, December 13, 1919, Baker, *Selected Letters*, pg. 19.
6. James R. Mellow, *Hemingway: A Life without Consequences* (New York: Houghton Mifflin Company, 1992), pg. 95.
7. Marcelline Hemingway to Grace Hemingway, August 31, 1919, Michael Reynolds, *Young Hemingway* (New York: Basil Blackwell, 1986), pg. 81.
8. *Ibid.*, pg. 92.

9. Matthew J. Bruccoli, ed., *Conversations with Ernest Hemingway* (Jackson: University of Mississippi Press, 1986), pg. 3.

10. Ralph Connable to EH, January 12, 1920, Hemingway Collection, John F. Kennedy Library, Boston.

11. EH to Jenkins, December 20, 1919, Baker, *Selected Letters*, pg. 29.

CHAPTER 1
Hemingway the Baby-sitter, 1920

1. Jeffrey Meyers, *Hemingway: A Biography* (New York: Harper & Row, 1985), pg. 48.

2. EH to Charles Fenton, October 9, 1952, Baker, *Selected Letter*, p. 786.

3. Clarence Hemingway to EH, February 17, 1920, Hemingway Collection.

4. EH to Fenton, October 9, 1952, Baker, *Selected Letters*, p. 786.

5. Dorothy Connable to Carlos Baker, April 17, 1964, McGeary Collection, *Toronto Star* Archives.

6. EH, *Eighty Eight Poems*, ed. Nicholas Gerogiannis, (New York: Harcourt Brace Jovanovich, 1979), p. 28.

7. Dorothy Connable to Baker, April 17, 1964, McGeary Collection.

8. Obituary of Ralph Connable Sr., *Toronto Star*, June 11, 1977.

9. Carlos Baker, *Ernest Hemingway: A Life Story* (New York: Charles Scribner's Sons, 1969), pg. 67.

CHAPTER 2
Just Another Hanger-on

1. Greg Clark, "Hemingway Slept Here," *Montreal Standard*, November 4, 1950.
2. *Ibid.*
3. *Ibid.*
4. *Toronto Star* Archives.
5. *Ibid.*
6. Ross Harkness, *J.E. Atkinson of The Star* (Toronto: University of Toronto Press, 1963), pg. 177.

CHAPTER 3
Half a Cent a Word

1. Clark, "Hemingway Slept Here."
2. *Ibid.*
3. J.H. Cranston, *Ink on My Fingers* (Toronto: The Ryerson Press, 1953), pg. 107.
4. Dorothy Connable to Baker, April 17, 1964, McGeary Collection.
5. McGeary Collection.
6. Dorothy Connable to Baker, April 17, 1964, McGeary Collection.
7. Baker, *Life Story*, pg. 67.

8. Dorothy Connable to Baker, April 17, 1964, McGeary Collection.

CHAPTER 4
The Sum Also Rises

1. Marceline Hemingway Sanford, *At the Hemingways: A Family Portrait* (Boston: Atlantic-Little Brown and Company, 1961) pg. 201.
2. Greg Clark to William McGeary, May 28, 1965, McGeary Collection.
3. Jimmy Cowan to William McGeary, undated, McGeary Collection.
4 J.H. Cranston, "Hemingway's Early Days," *Midland Free Press Herald*, October 19, 1945.
5. *Ibid.*
6. Harkness, *Atkinson of The Star*, pg. 156.
7. Jock Carroll, *The Life and Times of Greg Clark* (Toronto: Doubleday Canada, 1981), pg. 152.
8. Dorothy Connable to Baker, April 17, 1964, McGeary Collection.
9. Clarence Hemingway to EH, March 18, 1920, Hemingway Collection.

CHAPTER 5
Booze, Bass and Boxing

1. Michael Marrius, *Mr. Sam: The Life and Times of Samuel Bronfman* (Toronto: Viking, 1991), pg. 70.

2. Transcript of *Toronto Star* group interview of Hemingway colleagues, January 12, 1965, by William McGeary for Carlos Baker, *Toronto Star* Archives.

3. McGeary Collection.

4. EH, "Big Two-Hearted River: Part One," *The Complete Short Stories of Ernest Hemingway* (New York: Charles Scribner's Sons, 1987), pg. 161.

5. "Before You Go on a Canoe Trip, Learn Canoeing," *Toronto Star*, June 3, 1922.

6. EH, "Big Two-Hearted River: Part One," *Complete Short Stories*, pg. 161.

7. Baker, *Life Story*, pg. 68.

8. EH to Dorothy Connable, February 16, 1920, McGeary Collection.

9. Greg Clark to EH, June 25, 1920 [actually 1921], Hemingway Collection.

CHAPTER 6
A Ghostwriter Abroad, 1921

1. EH to Harriet Connable, June 1, 1920, Baker, *Selected Letters*, pg. 34.

2. EH to Charles Fenton, October 9, 1952, Baker, *Selected Letters*, pg. 786.

3. Clarence Hemingway to EH, June 4, 1920, Hemingway Collection.

4. Clarence Hemingway to Grace Hemingway, July 21, 1920, Leicester Hemingway, *My Brother Ernest Hemingway* (Cleveland: World, 1962), pg. 65.

5. Madelaine Hemingway Miller, *Ernie: Hemingway's Sister Sunny Remembers* (New York: Crown Publishers, 1975), pg. 67.

6. Mellow, *Life without Consequences*, pg. 119.

7. *Ibid.*

8. Reynolds, *Young Hemingway*, pgs. 137–38.

9. *Toronto Star* group interview.

10. *Ibid.*

11. *Ibid.*

12. Scott Donaldson, "Hemingway of the *Star*," *Ernest Hemingway: The Papers of a Writer*, ed. Bernard Oldsey (New York: Garland, 1981), pg. 90.

13. EH to John Bone, March 2, 1921, Hemingway Collection.

14. Bernice Kert, *The Hemingway Women* (New York: W.W. Norton, 1983), pg. 86.

15. Baker, *Life Story*, pg. 77.

16. *Ibid.*, pg. 78.

17. Hadley Richardson to EH, July 7, 1921, Hemingway Collection.

18. Donaldson, "Hemingway of the *Star*," pg. 90.

CHAPTER 7
Roving Reporter, 1922

1. Meyers, *Hemingway*, pg. 47.
2. EH, unpublished fragment, Hemingway Collection.
3. Meyers, *Hemingway*, pg. 94.

CHAPTER 8
Under the Influence

1. Scott Donaldson, *By Force of Will* (New York: Viking Press, 1977), pg. 245.
2. Meyers, *Hemingway*, pg. 82.
3. *Ibid.*, pg. 80.
4. EH, unpublished *Toronto Star* article, Hemingway Collection.
5. John Bone to EH, September 25, 1922, Hemingway Collection.
6. Donaldson, *By Force of Will*, pg. 245.
7. Meyers, *Hemingway*, pg. 98.
8. EH telegram to Frank Mason, December 15, 1922, Hemingway Collection.
9. Michael Reynolds, *Hemingway: The Paris Years* (Cambridge: Basil Blackwell, 1989), pg. 75.
10. Donaldson, "Hemingway of the *Star*, pg. 95.
11. EH, *A Moveable Feast* (New York: Charles Scribner's Sons, 1964), pg. 74.
12. Meyers, *Hemingway*, pg. 120.

13. EH to Clarence Hemingway, June 20, 1923, Hemingway Collection.
14. EH telegram to John Bone, May 9, 1923, Hemingway Collection.

CHAPTER 9
A Star Returns, 1923

1. John Bone to EH, August 18, 1923, Hemingway Collection.
2. Greg Clark to EH, August 31, 1923, Hemingway Collection.
3. Meyers, *Hemingway*, p. 122.
4. EH to Ezra Pound, September 6, 1923, Baker, *Selected Letters*, pg. 92.
5. Morley Callaghan, *That Summer in Paris* (New York: Penguin Books, 1963), pg. 25.
6. Roy Greenaway, *The News Game* (Toronto: Clarke, Irwin, 1966), pg. 10.
7. J.H. Cranston to Charles Fenton, August 7, 1951, *Apprenticeship*, pg. 272.
8. Fenton, *Apprenticeship*, pg. 245.
9. EH, unpublished *Toronto Star* article, Hemingway Collection.
10. EH memo to H.C. Hindmarsh, Item 682A, Hemingway Collection.
11. EH, "Search for Sudbury Coal a Gamble, Driller Tells of What He Has Found," *Toronto Star*, September 25, 1923.

12. Reynolds, *Hemingway: The Paris Years*, pg. 147.

CHAPTER 10
Disgrace Under Pressure

1. Callaghan, *That Summer In Paris*, pg. 26.
2. *Toronto Star* group interview.
3. EH, unpublished sketch, Hemingway Collection.
4. EH to Ezra Pound, October 13, 1923, Baker, *Selected Letters*, pg. 95.
5. Giola Diliberto, *Hadley* (New York: Ticknor & Fields, 1992), pg. 155.
6. EH to Gertrude Stein, October 11, 1923, Baker, *Selected Letters*, pg. 93.
7. *Ibid.*
8. Hadley to EH, October 8, 1923, Hemingway Collection.
9. McGeary Collection.
10. *Ibid.*
11. Diliberto, *Hadley*, pg. 159.

CHAPTER 11
Oh, Canada!

1. Diliberto, *Hadley*, pg. 159.
2. EH to Ezra Pound, October 13, 1923, Baker, *Selected Letters*, pg. 96.
3. Diliberto, *Hadley*, pg. 160.

4. EH to Ezra Pound, October 13, 1923, Baker, *Selected Letters*, pg. 95.

5. H.C. Hindmarsh memo to EH, Item 773E, Hemingway Collection.

6. H.C. Hindmarsh memo to EH, Item 723E, Hemingway Collection.

7. J.H. Cranston to Fenton, August 7, 1951, *Apprenticeship*, pg. 272.

8. EH, "Learns to Commune With the Fairies, Now Wins the $40,000 Nobel Prize," unsigned, *Toronto Star Weekly*, November 24, 1923.

9. EH to Sylvia Beach, November 6, 1923, Baker, *Selected Letters*, pg. 97.

10. EH to Gertrude Stein, November 9, 1923, Baker, *Selected Letters*, pg. 101.

CHAPTER 12
A Legend in the Making

1. Gertrude Stein, *The Autobiography of Alice B. Toklas* (New York: Harcourt, Brace and Company, 1933), p. 261.

2. Ezra Pound to EH, December 3, 1923, Hemingway Collection.

3. Meyers, *Hemingway*, pgs. 69–70.

4. EH to Edward O'Brien, November 20, 1923, Baker, *Selected Letters*, pg. 103.

5. *Ibid.*

6. *Toronto Star* group interview.

7. Callaghan, *That Summer in Paris*, pg. 27.

8. Callaghan, *That Summer in Paris*, pg. 28.

9. *Ibid.*, pg. 29.

10. *Ibid.*, pg. 30.

11. EH scrapbook, Hemingway Collection.

12. *Ibid.*

13. EH, *Complete Short Stories*, pg. 127.

14. Donaldson, *By Force of Will*, pgs. 242-243.

15. EH scrapbook, Hemingway Collection.

16. EH, handwritten notes, Hemingway Collection.

17. EH, unpublished sketch, Hemingway Collection.

CHAPTER 13
A Farewell to Toronto

1. Cranston, *Ink on My Fingers*, pg. 109.

2. *Toronto Star* group interview.

3. Gordon Sinclair, quoted in Denis Brian, *The True Gen* (New York: Grove Press, 1988), pg. 47.

4. EH to John Bone, undated, Hemingway Collection.

5. EH to John Bone, December 26, 1923, Hemingway Collection.

CHAPTER 14
Into the Sunrise, 1924

1. Grace Hemingway to EH, December 26, 1923, Hemingway Collection.

2. EH, "Up in Michigan," *Complete Short Stories*, pg. 59.
3. EH "Fathers and Sons," *Complete Short Stories*, pg. 369; Donaldson, *By Force of Will*, pg. 179.
4. Kenneth S. Lynn, *Hemingway*, (New York: Fawcett Columbine, 1987), pg. 225.
5. Callaghan, *That Summer in Paris*, pgs. 32–33.
6. Jimmy Cowan to William McGeary, undated, *Toronto Star* Archives.
7. Diliberto, *Hadley*, pg. 163.
8. Fenton, *Apprenticeship*, pg. 258.
9. EH, *The Transatlantic Review*, September 1924, pg. 300.
10. Fenton, *Apprenticeship*, pg. 262.

EPILOGUE
A Man of the World

1. Reynolds, *Hemingway: The Paris Years*, pg. 333.
2. Grace Hemingway to EH, February 20, 1927, Hemingway Collection.
3. EH, *A Moveable Feast*, pg. 210.
4. Diliberto, *Hadley*, pg. xiv.
5. Baker, *Life Story*, pg. 493
6. Cranston, *Ink on My Fingers*, pg. 110.
7. EH to Charles Fenton, January 12, 1952, Baker, *Selected Letters*, pg. 719.
8. Fenton, *Apprenticeship*, pg. 256.
9. Harkness, *Atkinson of the* Star, pg. 165.

INDEX